Cambridge Elements ≡

Elements in Perception
edited by
James T. Enns
The University of British Columbia

MULTISENSORY INTERACTIONS IN THE REAL WORLD

Salvador Soto-Faraco
Universitat Pompeu Fabra, Barcelona

Daria Kvasova
Universitat Pompeu Fabra, Barcelona

Emmanuel Biau
University of Birmingham

Nara Ikumi
Universitat Pompeu Fabra, Barcelona

Manuela Ruzzoli
Universitat Pompeu Fabra, Barcelona

Luis Morís-Fernández
Universitat Pompeu Fabra, Barcelona

Mireia Torralba
Universitat Pompeu Fabra, Barcelona

CAMBRIDGE
UNIVERSITY PRESS

CAMBRIDGE
UNIVERSITY PRESS

University Printing House, Cambridge CB2 8BS, United Kingdom

One Liberty Plaza, 20th Floor, New York, NY 10006, USA

477 Williamstown Road, Port Melbourne, VIC 3207, Australia

314–321, 3rd Floor, Plot 3, Splendor Forum, Jasola District Centre,
New Delhi – 110025, India

79 Anson Road, #06–04/06, Singapore 079906

Cambridge University Press is part of the University of Cambridge.

It furthers the University's mission by disseminating knowledge in the pursuit of
education, learning, and research at the highest international levels of excellence.

www.cambridge.org
Information on this title: www.cambridge.org/9781108468220
DOI: 10.1017/9781108578738

First published 2019

A catalogue record for this publication is available from the British Library.

ISBN 978-1-108-46822-0 Paperback
ISSN 2515-0502 (online)
ISSN 2515-0499 (print)

Multisensory Interactions in the Real World

Elements in Perception

DOI: 10.1017/9781108578738
First published online: August 2019

Salvador Soto-Faraco
Universitat Pompeu Fabra, Barcelona

Daria Kvasova
Universitat Pompeu Fabra, Barcelona

Emmanuel Biau
University of Birmingham

Nara Ikumi
Universitat Pompeu Fabra, Barcelona

Manuela Ruzzoli
Universitat Pompeu Fabra, Barcelona

Luis Morís-Fernández
Universitat Pompeu Fabra, Barcelona

Mireia Torralba
Universitat Pompeu Fabra, Barcelona

Author for correspondence: Salvador Soto-Faraco, salvador.soto@upf.edu

Abstract: The interactions between the senses are essential for cognitive functions such as perception, attention, and action planning. Past research helped understanding multisensory processes in the laboratory. Yet, the efforts to extrapolate these findings to the real-world are scarce. Extrapolation to real-world contexts is important for practical and theoretical reasons. Multisensory phenomena might be expressed differently in real-world settings compared to simpler laboratory situations. Some effects might become stronger, others may disappear, and new outcomes could be discovered. This Element discusses research that uncovers multisensory interactions in complex environments, with an emphasis on the interplay of multisensory mechanisms with other processes.

Keywords: multisensory, real-world, attention, perception, cognitive conflict

ISBNs: 9781108468220 (PB), 9781108578738 (OC)
ISSNs: 2515-0502 (online), ISSN 2515-0499 (print)

Contents

1 Introduction and Scope

The rich diversity of our sensory systems allows us to sample the environment from a variety of independent channels. Although the number of human senses is still under debate, it is undoubtedly far greater than the traditional five identified by Aristotle (Durie, 2005). The different senses, or sensory modalities, allow us to process complementary attributes of an object, extract correlations between its various features, and segregate some particular sensory properties from others. The impact of this multisensory capacity on cognition and brain functions has been extensively acknowledged in cognitive neuroscience literature. As multisensory processes have become a popular subject of scientific enquiry, they have also raised interest in other domains such as design, consumer sciences, philosophy, marketing, and even gastronomy. For example, at Hospital Sant Joan de Déu in Barcelona, researchers use multisensory principles to create more appetising menus for children undergoing chemotherapy, who often suffer taste alterations that lead to nutritional problems (Puigcerver et al., 2018).

One of the reasons for this surge of interest in multisensory processing is its relevance in understanding, explaining, and modulating human perception amidst the sensory complexity of real-world environments. Achieving this understanding would be difficult by studying each sense one at a time (e.g., Churchland, Ramachandran, & Sejnowski, 2005; De Gelder & Bertelson, 2003; Driver & Noesselt, 2008; Driver & Spence, 1998, 2000; Ernst & Banks, 2002; Ghazanfar & Schroeder, 2006; Macaluso & Driver, 2005; Shams & Seitz, 2008; Stein & Meredith, 1993). In contrast with this initial motivation, however, most of the research within the multisensory literature has used idealised, simplified laboratory tasks. The advantage of laboratory tasks is that they permit tight experimental control; that is to say, the phenomena under study can be carefully manipulated in the absence of extraneous variables that would complicate interpretation. The disadvantage, however, is that the deceptively simple models used in the laboratory are much unlike real-world environments. Because research in real-world-relevant conditions has been sparse, most basic laboratory findings in multisensory research, whilst valuable, have not been confirmed in ecologically valid conditions.

1.1 Why Is Real-World Cognitive Neuroscience Interesting?

There is ample agreement that generalising the findings discovered within controlled laboratory setups to real-life contexts faces substantial challenges. One of these challenges is the trade-off between rigorous experimental control and generalisation (ecological validity) (e.g., Blanton & Jaccard, 2006; Burgess et al., 2006; Kayser, Körding, & König, 2004; Kingstone et al., 2003; see also Neisser, 1976, 1982). In short, the higher the ecological validity of a study, the less the degree of experimental control that can be achieved over all relevant variables. So, if we are to trade experimental control for ecological validity, what is the gain of addressing real-world research?

One obvious motivation to address the generalisation of findings outside the laboratory is transference, viz. the application of basic principles discovered in experimental settings to practical problems. Transference has historically fuelled some multisensory studies to improve or assist human performance in real-life, multisensory tasks. For example, Sumby and Pollack's classic work, which demonstrated that watching a speaker's lips in a noisy environment enhances speech comprehension, was initially driven by the purely practical need of improving communication in industrial and military environments (Sumby & Pollack, 1954). The area of sensory substitution uses multisensory principles to induce cross-modal plasticity with the hope of improving perceptual capacities in sensory-deprived people (e.g., Bach-y-Rita & W. Kercel, 2003; Martolini et al., 2018; Vercillo, Tonelli, Goodale, & Gori, 2017). One example of this approach is a device called *BrainPort*, developed by Paul Bach-y-Rita. This device can transform visual shapes picked up by a video camera into tactile patterns presented to the tongue of blind persons, allowing them to perform some basic discrimination tasks (Bach-y-Rita, Danilov, Tyler, & Grimm, 2005; Danilov & Tyler, 2005). Other examples of multisensory approaches to practical problems are packaging design (Spence, 2016) and road safety (Ho, Reed, & Spence, 2007; Spence & Ho, 2008). In all these cases, the generalisation of basic laboratory findings is fundamental for the process of transference. Basic research must not only characterise multisensory phenomena by carefully controlled laboratory work and theoretical analysis, but it must also provide a good understanding of how these multisensory phenomena play out in complex, realistic environments (e.g., Maidenbaum & Abboud, 2014).

Besides practical motivations, there are also important theoretical and empirical lessons to be learned from extrapolating laboratory findings to real-world conditions. For one, as pointed out by E. A. Maguire, it would appear highly relevant to study the brain in the real-world conditions under which it has evolved to function (Maguire, 2012). These real-world conditions might disclose unforeseen gaps in our current knowledge, bring to the fore complex behaviours which might only occur (and therefore be studied) in these naturalistic settings, or even alter the outcomes of known laboratory-based results in significant ways (Hasson, Malach, & Heeger, 2010; Smilek, Birmingham, Cameron, Bischof, & Kingstone, 2006; Smilek,

Eastwood, Reynolds, & Kingstone, 2007). One example of how laboratory findings might change when tested under real-life conditions comes from visual attention research. Wolfe et al. (Wolfe, Horowitz, & Kenner, 2005) found that when people searched for easy-to-see but very infrequent targets (<1 per cent prevalence) under naturalistic conditions, such as guns in airport baggage screening, miss rates were unexpectedly high. Visual search is one of the most widely used psychophysical tasks in experimental psychology, but for practical reasons, the typical protocol, until Wolfe et al.'s study, had used high target prevalence (i.e., a large proportion of trials bear the target the observer is instructed to search for). In this case, even a modest step towards realistic scenarios, such as varying target prevalence, resulted in substantial changes in the outcome.

A further incentive to pursue real-world generalisation is to avoid the risk of atomisation; that is, laboratory approaches tend to isolate the object of study from all other possible confounding variables, sometimes neglecting the fact that studying isolated components of a complex system can obscure its emergent properties (Kitano, 2002; Ward, 2002). Brain mechanisms might be grossly mischaracterised when they are singled out in controlled laboratory experiments, compared to when they operate intertwined with each other in real-world conditions. For example, in the field of visual attention, the dissociation between endogenous and reflexive orienting mechanisms has been perpetuated by the mainstream use of idealised spatial cueing protocols. Endogenous orienting is often probed with central symbolic cues such as arrows, whereas exogenous orienting is usually triggered with eccentric salient cues such as lateralised flashes. Some studies, however, have highlighted that this strict dissociation between reflexive and endogenous attention protocols could prevent us from understanding attention orienting during everyday social interactions (Birmingham & Kingstone, 2009; Kingstone et al., 2003; Risko, Laidlaw, Freeth, Foulsham, & Kingstone, 2012).

The ability of human observers to find people amongst the complexity of real-world scenes provides another example of the potential risk of atomisation. Traditionally, visual attention research has emphasised a division between parallel feature-based search mechanisms (efficient) and serial conjunction search (inefficient). According to this classical framework, finding complex objects defined by the conjunction of various simple attributes requires an effortful, serial process. New findings emerging from search tasks in naturalistic scenes, however, show that finding people (fairly complex visual objects) in photos of cluttered and heterogeneous everyday life scenes is unexpectedly fast and efficient (Peelen & Kastner, 2014; Papeo, Groupil & Soto-Faraco, 2019).

1.2 Multisensory Processing in a Complex World

The 1990s saw increased motivation to study the interaction between the senses instead of each sense in isolation. This was in part because of a concern regarding ecological validity. It is our view, however, that this research did not go far enough in solving the concern. For the most part, efforts were directed towards understanding multisensory processes themselves. They were less concerned with understanding how these multisensory processes play out in real-world contexts or how they mesh with other brain processes under complex task demands. In real world conditions, multisensory interactions happen amidst, or even as part of, other processes such as attention, expectation, meaning integration, executive control, and sensorimotor integration. What transformations of multisensory phenomena discovered in simple environments will arise when they are brought to these more complex, close-to-real-life situations? Furthermore, which new questions might emerge from studying these scenarios?

The interest in approaching real-world conditions in multisensory research is now taking off (e.g., Mastroberardino, Santangelo, & Macaluso, 2015; Matusz, Dikker, Huth, & Perrodin, 2018; Nardo, Santangelo, & Macaluso, 2014). This new interest is not unique to multisensory research. It sparked investigations in other fields such as spatial navigation (Spiers & Maguire, 2006), episodic memory (e.g., Santangelo, Di Francesco, Mastroberardino, & Macaluso, 2015), event perception (e.g., Hasson, Nir, Levy, Fuhrmann, & Malach, 2004), and sensorimotor decision making (e.g., Gallivan, Chapman, Wolpert, & Flanagan, 2018), as well as in the visuospatial attention domain as we mentioned earlier (Kingstone et al., 2003; Nardo, Santangelo, & Macaluso, 2011; Peelen & Kastner, 2014). In the case of multisensory perception, the knowledge gap between laboratory and real life is still significant. For example, although there is a sizable body of evidence for cross-modal enhancement (i.e., perception in one sensory modality is more accurate and faster when complementary information is available in another modality), the impact of this multisensory benefit in real-world conditions is still largely unknown. Based on the examples from visual research discussed above, one can infer that understanding the interplay between multisensory processes and other mechanisms under complex conditions would appear to be important.

Unfortunately, multisensory effects discovered in the laboratory are rarely put to the test under real-life conditions. These tests are not only difficult to realise, and unfeasible in some cases, but very often their data is hard to interpret. As a compromise solution, some studies addressing intermediate steps between laboratory and real-life conditions have begun to emerge. This is referred to as 'naturalistic laboratory research' (by Matusz et al., 2018). This Element brings up some examples from the multisensory literature in which known laboratory findings have been put to the test in complex situations, i.e., when multisensory mechanisms are studied in interaction with other cognitive processes. The focus will be placed on the interplay between multisensory processes and attention, prediction, temporal organisation, and conflict processing mechanisms. These illustrative examples have a bias towards the authors' own research interests and are mostly confined to human studies with healthy, young adults. Other ramifications of multisensory research, which might also be relevant to real-world generalisation, are left out of this review. (More extensive reviews about multisensory processes can be found, for example, in Calvert, Spence, & Stein, 2004; Spence, 2018; and Stein, 2012.)

We will first consider the issue of the limited capacity of human information-processing machinery. Sensory-rich, complex scenarios, typical of real-life environments, pose a serious problem of selection to the limited-capacity cognitive system (e.g., Desimone & Duncan, 1995; Huang, Treisman, & Pashler, 2007). The term *selective attention* generally refers to a variety of processes and mechanisms that help select, parse, and organise information in order to allocate resources efficiently. The interplay between these attention mechanisms and multisensory processes lies at the core of any attempt to address perception in real-world environments. Do multisensory interactions break down under such high selection pressure? This issue has been the object of intense debate in the last few years (De Meo, Murray, Clarke, & Matusz, 2015; Hartcher-O'Brien, Soto-Faraco, & Adam, 2017; Hartcher-O'Brien et al., 2016; Koelewijn, Bronkhorst, & Theeuwes, 2010; Navarra, Alsius, Soto-Faraco, & Spence, 2010; Talsma, Senkowski, Soto-Faraco, & Woldorff, 2010; ten Oever et al., 2016). Section 2 presents a brief up-to-date review of this debate with a focus on complex, real-world scenarios.

Next, we will discuss the impact of prediction and temporal organisation in parsing complex, multisensory environments. Real-world environments are often structured across various scales, from the smallest spatial and temporal patterns to an intricate web of semantic relationships. Multisensory perception exploits this structure via several mechanisms that help anticipate and organise sensory inputs. These mechanisms can involve phase reset, entrainment of neural activity to rhythmic sensory input (Lakatos, Chen, O'Connell, Mills, & Schroeder, 2007; Schroeder & Lakatos, 2009), grouping events in time (Ikumi & Soto-Faraco, 2014; Lewald & Guski, 2003; Vatakis & Spence, 2006), anticipating properties from one modality to another via semantic association (Chen & Spence, 2010, 2011; Iordanescu, Guzman-Martinez, Grabowecky, & Suzuki, 2008; Parise & Spence, 2009), and inferring causal structure between sensory inputs via priors built from experience (Gau & Noppeney, 2016; Kayser & Shams, 2015; Noppeney & Lee, 2018). Section 3 discusses some examples of prediction and temporal organisation in multisensory processing and their potential consequences for real-world perception.

Third and lastly, we will consider the interplay between multisensory interactions and conflict processing mechanisms. Brain mechanisms of conflict processing are set in motion when incompatible mental representations are activated and compete (Botvinick, Braver, Barch, Carter, & Cohen, 2001). We will discuss two examples of this interplay. The first example regards sensorimotor conflict; that is, when alternative courses of action in response to a stimulus compete to drive behaviour. This kind of conflict can arise when events in different sensory modalities trigger alternative spatial representations for action. The second example of the interplay between multisensory and conflict processes relates to perception of inter-sensory conflict. Multisensory research has frequently resorted to inter-sensory conflict as a model to study general principles of multisensory integration (Bertelson, 1998; De Gelder & Bertelson, 2003) even though most real-world objects provide congruent (i.e., correlated) information across the senses. Therefore, it is surprising that the relationship between multisensory and conflict processes has rarely been addressed explicitly. Section 4 presents some recent findings that bring to the fore the interplay between conflict mechanisms and multisensory interactions.

2 Multisensory Processing and Attention: Real-World Environments Require a Multifaceted Interplay

Imagine a stranger coming to talk to you at a party at the precise moment when the buzz is at its loudest. The hearing is tough, so to figure out what the stranger is trying to say you must listen carefully while watching his lip movements. In this case, the effort of integrating visual and auditory information demands our fully devoted attention. In other cases, however, multisensory interactions appear to happen in an effortless, unavoidable fashion. An instance of this is when the olfactory and gustatory properties of foods create the unified experience of taste. When do we need to focus attention to capitalise on the benefits of multisensory interactions, and when do these benefits arise effortlessly? The relationship between attention and multisensory interactions has been in the limelight for nearly two decades (Alsius, Navarra, Campbell, & Soto-Faraco, 2005; Busse, Roberts, Crist, Weissman, & Woldorff, 2005; De Gelder & Bertelson, 2003; Driver, 1996; McDonald, Teder-Sälejärvi, & Ward, 2001; Spence & Driver, 2004; Talsma et al., 2010).

Early views regarding the relationship between multisensory processes and attention were positioned along two opposing extremes. At one end of the spectrum were researchers who regarded multisensory processes as automatic and pre-attentive. At the other end of the spectrum were researchers who emphasised the need for selective attention as a prerequisite for multisensory integration. Under the former view, multisensory integration does not only happen irrespective of whether the involved sensory inputs are attended or not, but its outcome can summon attention itself (Bertelson, Vroomen, De Gelder, & Driver, 2000; Driver, 1996; Van Der Burg, Olivers, Bronkhorst, & Theeuwes, 2008; Vroomen, Bertelson, & de Gelder, 2001). Under the latter view, however, attentional selection must be deployed prior to (and often is a condition for) multisensory integration (Alsius, Navarra, Campbell, & Soto-Faraco, 2005; Duncan, Martens, & Ward, 1997; Talsma & Woldorff, 2005). These opposing views often put the emphasis on different conceptions about the functional architecture of multisensory interactions in the brain. Feedforward architectures allow bottom-up convergence of sensory information, which is associated with fast and automatic interactions. In contrast, feedback (or recurrent) architectures are amenable to attention mediation via top-down processes (Driver & Noesselt, 2008; Driver & Spence, 2000; Foxe & Schroeder, 2005).

2.1 The Real-World Relevance of the Interplay between Attention and Multisensory Processes

The either–or debate about the role of attention in multisensory processes sketched above has important implications for real-world perception (Hartcher-O'Brien et al., 2017, 2016; Koelewijn et al., 2010; Matusz et al., 2018; Talsma, 2015; Talsma et al., 2010; ten Oever et al., 2016). If we accept the hypothesis that multisensory interactions occur automatically, in a purely bottom-up fashion, then multisensory phenomena discovered under simplified laboratory conditions should still work well in more complex real-world scenarios. In this case, multisensory interactions can bring about very relevant benefits[1] without any cognitive cost. If, on the other hand, we reject the

---

[1] For example, automatic integration mechanisms can furnish multisensory events with increased salience (Noesselt et al., 2010; Van Der Burg et al., 2008), leading to faster and more precise saccadic reactions to imperative events in the environment (Colonius & Arndt, 2001; Corneil, Van Wanrooij, Munoz, & Van Opstal, 2002; Diederich & Colonius, 2004); improve sensitivity to stimuli that are hard to notice (Caclin et al., 2011; Frassinetti et al., 2002; Gleiss & Kayser, 2013, 2014; Jaekl & Harris, 2009; Jaekl & Soto-Faraco, 2010; Noesselt et al., 2010); increase precision when estimating the properties of objects (Ernst & Banks, 2002; Fetsch, Pouget, DeAngelis, & Angelaki, 2012; Yau, Olenczak, Dammann, & Bensmaia, 2009); and make perception in noisy environments more accurate (Grant & Seitz, 2000; Jaekl et al., 2015; Ross, Saint-Amour, Leavitt, Javitt, & Foxe, 2006; Sumby & Pollack, 1954).

automaticity hypothesis, the complexity of real-world conditions might impose strong limitations on, if not compromise altogether, the multisensory phenomena discovered under simpler laboratory conditions. In this case, attentional selection can become a bottleneck to achieving the perceptual benefits of multisensory interactions.

Research findings offering evidence for automatic multisensory interactions have been matched by equally compelling results supporting attentional mediation. According to recent reviews on the topic, both types of mechanism do play a role, and the debate has boiled down to a more nuanced question: what is the balance of power between bottom-up automatic processes and top-down mediation (De Meo et al., 2015; Hartcher-O'Brien et al., 2016; Talsma, 2015; ten Oever et al., 2016)? The answer to this question seems to depend on a variety of factors, including the level(s) of processing involved in the representation of a multisensory event (from low-level spatio-temporal attributes to higher-level semantic properties), the physical salience and task-relevance of the stimuli, and the perceptual load[2] of the scenario, amongst others. Similar to what was proposed in the biased competition framework of attention a couple of decades ago (Desimone & Duncan, 1995), the outcome of multisensory interactions might emerge from a competitive process between bottom-up evidence and top-down, endogenous biases.

One study by Fujisaki and colleagues (Fujisaki, Koene, Arnold, Johnston, & Nishida, 2006) provides a demonstration of this competition between bottom-up and top-down processes during multisensory perception. Participants saw a display populated by blobs flashing randomly plus a sound varying in amplitude. They had to find the only blob whose flashing was synchronised with the amplitude changes of the sound. Hence, subjects were to individuate the one audiovisually congruent object amongst other visual-only distractors. Fujisaki et al. discovered that search efficiency for audiovisual synchrony was determined both by exogenous factors, triggering bottom-up interactions, as well as by endogenous processes relying on top-down mediation. Audiovisual targets whose single-modality components were salient (by making them spatially and temporally unique) could be detected automatically. When the salience of single-modality components was reduced because the inputs were embedded in more cluttered displays, endogenous attention became necessary for the detection of audiovisual synchrony. A similar outcome was obtained with speaking faces and speech sounds in subsequent experiments, which will be discussed later in the context of language (Alsius & Soto-Faraco, 2011).

---

[2] Perceptual load relates to the number of different items in a display that need to be perceived and/ or the amount of resources required for the perceptual identification of each item.

The competition involving stimulus-driven bottom-up processes and endogenously driven top-down biases can play out throughout the different levels of representation that characterise multisensory objects (e.g., spatial location, temporal correspondence, semantics, action plans). This framework of competition at multiple stages, called 'multifaceted interplay' (Talsma et al., 2010), can be especially suitable to understand multisensory interactions in complex scenarios; that is, scenarios where goal-directed behaviours likely involve parsing information at various levels of representation in a high-load, but structured environment. The multifaceted interplay hypothesis can account for the fact that sometimes multisensory processes occur in a bottom-up, automatic manner, even influencing attention, whereas at other times multisensory processes are mediated by attention. That is, attention and multisensory interactions can mutually influence each other or at times even be indistinguishable from each other. Below we discuss the evidence for either type of influence, with some examples relevant to real-world multisensory perception.

2.2 What, and How Much, Can We Expect from Bottom-Up Multisensory Interactions?

One recurrent finding supporting an automatic view of multisensory interactions is that a multisensory singleton embedded amongst unisensory events stands out and can therefore capture attention. The straightforward interpretation of this type of finding is that correlated sensory inputs are automatically bound into a multisensory representation, increasing the salience of that object in the scene by making it unique. For example, it has been claimed that a sound synchronised with a visual event can make it seem brighter[3] (Stein, London, Wilkinson, & Price, 1996), last longer (Vroomen & Gelder, 2000), and make it easier to detect (Andersen & Mamassian, 2008; Bolognini, Frassinetti, Serino, & Làdavas, 2005; Frassinetti et al., 2002; Jaekl & Soto-Faraco, 2010) and faster to respond to (e.g., Murray et al., 2005; Pérez-Bellido, Soto-Faraco, & López-Moliner, 2013). A popular study by Van der Burg et al. (Van Der Burg et al., 2008) showed that in crowded dynamic visual search displays, a spatially uninformative sound synchronised with an irrelevant colour change led to pop-out in an otherwise difficult serial search task. This phenomenon has been dubbed the 'pip and pop'. Similarly, Maddox et al. (Maddox, Atilgan, Bizley, & Lee, 2015) showed that irrelevant visual events could aid auditory selective attention. Some of these phenomena have been linked to physiological interactions in subcortical or primary sensory areas – defined as 'early', sensory-based interaction (Driver & Noesselt, 2008; Shams & Kim, 2010; Stein & Stanford, 2008).

---

[3] This interpretation, however, has been disputed (Odgaard, Arieh, & Marks, 2003).

Complementing the results discussed above, Santangelo and Spence (2007) reported that multisensory events are less prone to be neglected in high-perceptual-load conditions than are unisensory events. This result could be explained by an automaticity account whereby multisensory interactions occur via bottom-up mechanisms based on a feedforward architecture. Some neuroimaging findings support this view because they reveal that the brain correlates of multisensory interactions can be expressed at early stages of sensory processing, in terms of both latency and functional anatomy (Foxe et al., 2000; Matusz & Eimer, 2011; Molholm et al., 2002; Murray et al., 2005; Van der Burg, Talsma, Olivers, Hickey, & Theeuwes, 2011). Some authors have related these fast, automatic multisensory interactions to the discovery of direct (i.e., monosynaptic) cortico-cortical connections between sensory areas of different modalities (Falchier, Clavagnier, Barone, & Kennedy, 2002; Rockland & Ojima, 2003).

2.2.1 Multisensory Warning and Interference in Real-World Environments

The putative automaticity of multisensory enhancement effects, such as the ones described above, conveys a 'privileged' attentional status to multisensory stimuli. This has potential real-life implications for the design of warning signals in demanding environments. For example, multisensory events appear to be effective at summoning the drivers' attention to road hazards, eliciting fast braking responses (Ho et al., 2007; Spence & Santangelo, 2009). Remarkably, some findings suggest that the capacity of multisensory events for attracting attention is not limited solely to spatio-temporal congruence between abrupt stimulus onsets (typical flash-beep stimuli). They indicate, as well, that this multisensory benefit extends to cross-modal congruence between higher-level attributes such as semantics (Iordanescu, Grabowecky, Franconeri, Theeuwes, & Suzuki, 2010; Iordanescu, Grabowecky, & Suzuki, 2011; Iordanescu et al., 2008; Pesquita, Brennan, Enns, & Soto-Faraco, 2013). This research shows that finding one predefined visual target object (e.g., cell-phone) amongst other ordinary everyday life objects is faster if the person hears its characteristic sound (e.g., ringtone). This could have important implications for real-life contexts, where we are usually surrounded by familiar objects interconnected by a rich web of semantic associations. This case will be addressed further in Section 3.3. In other cases, applied research concerning real-world scenarios (e.g., in the context of driving) has concentrated on the potential consequences of synergy or interference when a variety of spatial cues are delivered to different sensory modalities (Ho & Spence, 2014; Spence & Ho, 2015b, 2015a, Spence & Soto-Faraco, in press).

2.2.2 Multisensory Integration vs. Interaction

A subtle but important question is whether or not multisensory interactions can be explained by general-purpose brain mechanisms, that is, mechanisms that do not involve machinery specifically devoted to integration between sensory modalities (McDonald et al., 2001; van Atteveldt, Murray, Thut, & Schroeder, 2014). According to this view, the mechanisms benefitting from complementary inputs in different sensory modalities are not fundamentally different from the known mechanisms that capitalise on multiple cues from the same modality.

For example, some cross-modal interactions occurring at short latencies could be due to exogenous attention cueing (temporal or spatial) or alerting (Andersen & Mamassian, 2008; Jaekl, Pérez-Bellido, & Soto-Faraco, 2014; Lippert, Logothetis, & Kayser, 2007; Pérez-Bellido et al., 2013; see Pápai & Soto-Faraco, 2017 for a similar argument using stimuli presented below the threshold of awareness). Other cross-modal interactions can be explained with statistical models based on the redundancy between independent information channels (Miller, 1982; Pannunzi et al., 2015; Quick, 1974). Because these processes are not specifically multisensory (they happen via mechanisms that operate within as well as across modalities), and their effects are often reducible to linear combinations like the ones described by redundancy statistical models, one does not need to assume any specific multisensory mechanism to explain them (see Pannunzi et al., 2015, for discussion). Some of the phenomena discussed in the previous section as examples of bottom-up multisensory processes could be described in this way.

In this Element, the expression *multisensory interaction* will be used as an all-inclusive term referring to any cross-modal influence. This term encompasses multisensory effects that are based on general-purpose brain mechanisms (e.g., alerting processes and statistical redundancy effects) as well as effects that are based on specific cross-modal convergence mechanisms. The term *multisensory integration*, instead, will be reserved for the latter case; that is, when the process relies on machinery that is specifically multisensory. This includes, for example, multisensory convergence mechanisms and/or effects whose outcome is not reducible to statistical redundancy. In such cases, multisensory events elicit behavioural or neural responses that cannot be predicted by linear models based on combining unisensory responses (e.g., Colonius & Diederich, 2004; Laurienti, Kraft, Maldjian, Burdette, & Wallace, 2004; Maddox et al., 2015; Molholm et al., 2002; Murray et al., 2005; Senkowski, Talsma, Herrmann, & Woldorff, 2005; Talsma, Doty, & Woldorff, 2006). Particular examples of *multisensory integration* are found in animal physiology, where superadditive

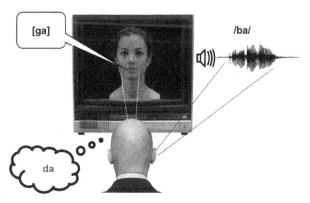

Figure 1 The McGurk effect is a laboratory-based cross-modal illusion whereby the listener hears a syllable different from the one that has actually been said. This happens when the sound of a syllable (e.g., 'ba') is dubbed onto the video clip of a speaker whose lips silently articulate a different syllable (e.g., 'ga'). In this case, the listener will frequently experience hearing the syllable 'da', which is a phonemic compromise between the speech sound and what the lips articulate. The McGurk illusion can be created with other speech fragments, such as words, and even whole sentences, but it will work with only some specific combinations of phonemes, such as the ones in the example.

responses have been described in multisensory neurons of the superior colliculus (Stein & Stanford, 2008). Multisensory integration outcomes have also been reported in human behaviour. For example, some studies have found that the concurrent presentation of subthreshold smell and taste stimuli can create a suprathreshold sensation (Dalton, Doolittle, Nagata, & Breslin, 2000). Other studies have found that reaction times for cross-modal stimulus detection are significantly faster than the prediction of redundancy models (Murray et al., 2005; but see Otto & Mamassian, 2012; Pannunzi et al., 2015, for alternative explanations). Additional cases of multisensory integration can be inferred from cross-modal enhancements that are tuned to specific feature values (e.g., Lunghi & Alais, 2013; Pérez-Bellido et al., 2013) and from cross-modal enhancement by a subsequent (instead of preceding) events (e.g., Andersen & Mamassian, 2008; Leone & McCourt, 2013; Miller, 1986). Particularly compelling demonstrations of multisensory integration are multisensory illusions such as the McGurk effect.[4] In this case, the perception elicited by a cross-modal stimulus is different from either of its unisensory components (see Figure 1).

---

[4] Demonstrations of the ventriloquist illusion and the McGurk effect can be found following this link: www.upf.edu/web/mrg/demos

2.3 What Multisensory Interactions Are Mediated by Top-Down Attention (and to What Extent)?

Not all instances of multisensory interaction seem to persist in complex, attentionally demanding situations, akin to those in real-life environments. In fact, a fair number of findings show that multisensory interactions occur to a lesser extent, or not at all, when attention is pulled away from the relevant sensory inputs (e.g., Andersen, Tiippana, Laarni, Kojo, & Sams, 2009; Fairhall & Macaluso, 2009; Morís Fernández, Visser, Ventura-Campos, Ávila, & Soto-Faraco, 2015; Senkowski et al., 2005; Talsma & Woldorff, 2005). In support of this idea, Talsma and Woldorff (2005; see also Senkowski et al., 2005) found that the ERP correlates of multisensory integration weaken if the multisensory event appears at an unattended location. Other studies have measured behavioural and neural correlates of multisensory interactions when resources available to process the multisensory event are compromised in dual-task or high-perceptual-load protocols. Several experiments following this approach have used the McGurk effect as a proxy for multisensory integration and have shown that this multisensory illusion weakens when attention is directed away from the stimulus (Alsius, Möttönen, Sams, Soto-Faraco, & Tiippana, 2014; Alsius et al., 2005; Alsius, Navarra, & Soto-Faraco, 2007; Sams, Tiippana, Puharinen, & Möttönen, 2011; Tiippana, Andersen, & Sams, 2004).

Besides experiments using direct manipulations of attention, other studies have revealed top-down modulations of multisensory interactions by measuring multisensory perception while manipulating task goals, context, and prior experience (Donohue, Green, & Woldorff, 2015; Gau & Noppeney, 2016; Nahorna, Berthommier, & Schwartz, 2012). One example of contextual modulation of multisensory perception is a study conducted by Nahorna and collaborators (2012). In Nahorna et al.'s study, observers were shown McGurk stimuli after watching a few seconds either of normal audiovisually congruent speech or of audiovisually mismatched speech fragments. The very same McGurk stimulus was more likely to produce the illusion (a proxy for multisensory integration) in the former case than in the latter.

Another symptom of top-down mediation of multisensory interactions is that task-irrelevant, unattended, multisensory events often fail to capture attention. For example, Matusz et al. (2015) found that unisensory (auditory) distractors interfered as much as multisensory audiovisual distractors using a flanker response competition task (see also Lunn, Sjoblom, Ward, Soto-Faraco, & Forster, 2019). Though evidence for interference from irrelevant multisensory distractors exists, it is generally weaker than the evidence for facilitation effects from relevant (attended) multisensory events (Iordanescu et al., 2011; Matusz & Eimer, 2011; Van Der Burg et al., 2008).

In sum, there is mounting evidence that the expression of multisensory interactions can be strongly limited when tested in complex environments. These limitations are discussed below in relationship to real-world perception.

2.3.1 Multisensory Interactions in Cluttered Environments Need Top-Down Attention

As outlined in the introduction, real-world contexts are often characterised by rich, dynamic, and sensory diverse scenarios which typically unfold in a time scale of seconds or minutes (Hasson et al., 2010). How does our brain tell, in such situations, whether sensory coincidences arise from a common event (and therefore are potentially conducive of multisensory interactions) or if they are just spurious correlations? In essence, what is to be integrated out of all the possible sensory combinations out there? This question has been addressed in various studies where participants were asked to find cross-modally matching events in multisensory, cluttered environments (e.g., Alsius & Soto-Faraco, 2011; Fujisaki, Koene, Arnold, Johnston, & Nishida, 2006; Fujisaki & Nishida, 2010; Kösem & van Wassenhove, 2012; Maddox et al., 2015; van de Par & Kohlrausch, 2004). Generally, the results of these studies support the notion that cross-modally congruent events do not stand out in cluttered scenarios.

Alsius and Soto-Faraco (2011) provided a demonstration of this result with relevance to real life. Their study showed that one audiovisual talking face (lips matching with speech sounds) failed to pop out when embedded amongst an array of other silent talking faces. These findings stand in apparent contrast with the results outlined in Section 2.1 supporting the bottom-up nature of multi-sensory interactions, such as the pip-and-pop effect and auditory enhancement by vision (Maddox et al., 2015; Van Der Burg et al., 2008). To reconcile both sets of findings, one must resort to the role of salient events, as suggested by the multifaceted interplay hypothesis in Talsma et al. (Talsma et al., 2010; Van der Burg et al., 2011). In the pip-and-pop effect and similar phenomena, the accessory stimulus (in the irrelevant modality) provides a salient unisensory singleton that can be quickly encoded for binding to simultaneous events in relevant modalities, even when less salient. This would be like the sudden blare of an ambulance siren, which automatically triggers the binding of other spatially and temporally matching sensory features (e.g., colour, shape, direction of motion of the ambulance) to one individual vehicle representation, even in the most crowded street. In the absence of such salient unisensory landmarks that summon attention in the first place, multisensory interactions seem to require top-down selection.

Going back to the loud party example that opened this section, one popular laboratory task with real-life relevance is auditory selective attention to one conversation amongst others going on at the same time. This is famously known as the 'cocktail party' problem[5] (e.g., Bronkhorst, 2000; Cherry, 1953). The multisensory version of this problem is equally relevant, if not more so, in real-life settings; namely, whether watching visual information from the speaker's lips improves auditory selective attention. Earlier results from Driver (Driver, 1996) would suggest that this is the case, although the reliability of this finding was later disputed (Jack, O'Shea, Cottrell, & Ritter, 2013). The results of an experiment by Alsius et al. (Alsius & Soto-Faraco, 2011) provide a qualified answer; in multi-speaker scenarios, one speech stream can be singled out from several others by watching its corresponding lips, but localising the source of the sound requires attentional control; that is, the sight of articulatory gestures may aid selection of the corresponding auditory message amongst distracters, but to a limited extent. These results partly confirm the conclusions suggested in Maddox et al. (2015).

A final argument against the automaticity of multisensory processes in real-life scenarios could be put forth; if multisensory interactions were indeed automatic and unavoidable, then irrelevant multisensory events going on in complex scenarios should constantly interfere with performance regarding relevant events. This does not seem to be the case, however. Although some results suggest that voluntarily shifting attention away from a congruent but irrelevant audiovisual speech stream involves some cost (Driver & Spence, 1994), most findings show that this interference is rather modest in high-perceptual-load or divided attention conditions (Duncan et al., 1997; Morís Fernández et al., 2015; Soto-Faraco, Morein-Zamir, & Kingstone, 2005).

2.3.2 Neural Expression of Multisensory Interactions in Cluttered Environments

In line with the behavioural findings just discussed, there is complementary evidence suggesting that the neural expression of multisensory interactions in cluttered, dynamic contexts is top-down regulated (Fairhall & Macaluso, 2009; Morís Fernández et al., 2015; Senkowski, Saint-Amour, Gruber, & Foxe, 2008; Zion Golumbic et al., 2013). Fairhall & Macaluso (2009) devised an fMRI experiment where subjects watched two pairs of speaking lips (presented side

---

[5] This YouTube link contains a demonstration of the 'multisensory' cocktail party problem: https://youtu.be/mN–nV61gDo

by side) while hearing one voice at the same time. BOLD responses (a measure of brain activity) in the superior temporal sulcus (STS: a well-known multisensory brain area) were stronger when visual spatial attention was covertly directed to the lips that corresponded to the voice, as compared to when attention was directed away from the congruent lips. The second finding in Fairhall and Macaluso's study was that attention not only modulated responses in multisensory brain areas but also had an impact on brain activity in early unisensory areas (such as the occipital visual cortex). This finding substantiates earlier claims regarding functional architectures based on feedback, which propose that multisensory interactions involve top-down modulation of sensory areas (Driver & Noesselt, 2008; Macaluso & Driver, 2005; Macaluso, Frith, & Driver, 2000). An EEG study using a similar multi-speaker selective attention task (Senkowski et al., 2008) arrived at similar conclusions. In this study, participants watched three side-by-side speaking faces and were asked to selectively attend the central one. Senkowski et al. found that the amplitude of the EEG signal induced by irrelevant speaking faces correlated with the degree of behavioural interference they produced on selective listening performance.

Although Fairhall and Macaluso's (2009) and Senkowki et al.'s (2008) studies approached the complexity of real-life speech perception in multispeaker scenarios, they used lists of syllables or isolated words as stimuli. This approach is convenient for control but removes many critical linguistic components of naturalistic speech (i.e., prosody, syntax, and integrated semantics). In a further step towards real-life relevance, Zion-Golumbic et al. (2013) measured MEG responses to continuous natural speech from two side-by-side speaking faces together with their corresponding sounds. One of their key results was that MEG responses to the speech envelope in the auditory cortex were regulated as a function of which speaker was attended, over and beyond responses to auditory-alone speech. More recently, Morís-Fernández et al. (2015) measured BOLD responses in an fMRI study using similar, naturalistic speech conditions (see Figure 2). In this case, one single talking face was presented for a few seconds together with two overlapping speech streams, all presented at the same time and from the same location. One of the two speech streams matched the talking face. Brain responses to this stimulus changed dramatically depending on whether participants' auditory attention was selectively focused on the speech stream matching the speakers' lips versus the mismatching one. This modulation happened even though the multisensory event presented to the subjects was physically identical across conditions; that is, the only source of the effect was their focus of attention. As in Fairhall and Macaluso (2009), in Morís-Fernández et al. (2015) BOLD responses were

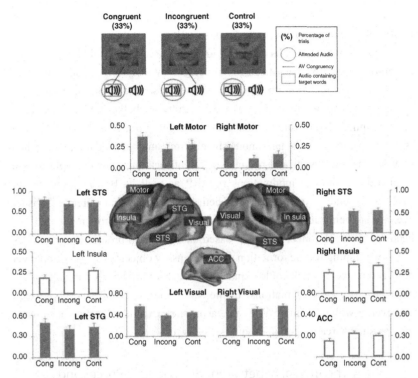

Figure 2 Top: schematic depiction of the conditions in Morís-Fernández et al., 2015. The congruent and incongruent conditions (used for the BOLD contrast depicted below) are identical. Both contained two speech streams from one overlapping central location (here depicted separately for clarity) plus a visible talking face whose lips matched one of the two voices. The only difference between conditions in this experiment was that attention could be directed either to the voice congruent with the lips or to the one incongruent with the lips. A further control condition was included in which neither of the two speech streams matched the central lips. Bottom: Significant BOLD change (the bar plots depict the Beta parameter in arbitrary units) for the contrast congruent minus incongruent (hot colours / solid bars refer to positive differences, cold colours / empty bars to negative differences). The results include BOLD increase in areas associated with audiovisual integration of congruent audiovisual speech (STS, STG, and motor areas), in areas related to visual processing (occipital cortex), and BOLD decrease in regions associated with processing conflicting information (ACC, Insula).

down-regulated in multisensory association areas when attending away from the audiovisually congruent speech event. Furthermore, responses were also down-regulated in the visual cortex under these conditions. These findings provide additional support to the idea that feedback to sensory areas regulates multisensory interactions via top-down selection.

The neuroimaging results discussed in this section so far could be catalogued as top-down gating of multisensory processes by attention. Another form of attention mediation of multisensory processes in sensory-rich scenarios is the so-called 'spread of attention' (Busse et al., 2005; Fiebelkorn, Foxe, Schwartz, & Molholm, 2010). In short, attention to an event in one sensory modality can 'spread' to encompass synchronous signals from another modality, even when they are task-irrelevant and occur at different locations. For example, Busse et al. (2005) showed modulations of ERP as well as BOLD responses to irrelevant sounds as a function of whether concurrent (but unrelated) visual events were being attended or not. This attentional spread across modalities has been suggested to reflect an object-based, late selection process that promotes sensory grouping for the formation of multisensory objects. This is a simple yet powerful concept which could explain the effects of attention on the formation of multisensory representations. In the same line as the pip-and-pop effect, however, it would be interesting to measure the extent to which event salience mediates the spreading of attention mechanism.

2.4 The Interplay between Multisensory Processing and Attention in Real-World Scenes

Although most of the studies discussed above are still far from being ecologically valid, they have helped identify various sources of regulation acting upon multisensory interactions in complex, demanding tasks. Understanding how all these components fit together when the perceptual system operates under naturalistic, real-life conditions can pose a serious challenge (see Bordier, Puja, & Macaluso, 2013; Cavallina, Puccio, Capurso, Bremner, & Santangelo, 2018; Macaluso & Doricchi, 2013; and Nardo, Console, Reverberi, & Macaluso, 2016 for examples using visual-only scenes). This challenge has rarely been addressed. An observational study by Rummukainen et al. (Rummukainen, Radun, Virtanen, & Pulkki, 2014) attempted to characterise the perceptual attributes that are subjectively relevant in naturalistic audiovisual environments. They recorded short video clips of everyday life scenes in Helsinki and reproduced them in an immersive environment covering the whole visual and auditory fields around the viewer. Rummukainen et al. used a similarity rating task and semi-structured interviews to find out which attributes could explain the categorisation of the scenes extracted from the participant's responses. Their results, albeit at an exploratory stage, highlight the importance of the interplay between the physical salience of attributes at a single-modality level (such as visual movement or acoustic noisiness) and more conceptual, supra-modal features related to the semantics of the scene (e.g., calm, pleasant).

Nardo et al. (2014) reported one of the few fMRI studies to address the interaction between bottom-up and top-down aspects of multisensory processing in realistic scenes. Eye-gaze data and BOLD responses were recorded while participants watched short video clips from everyday life scenes, with the corresponding sounds of the events therein. BOLD responses were mainly associated with visual and auditory salience reflected in classically defined sensory brain areas (occipital cortex and superior temporal cortex, for visual and auditory salience, respectively) as well as in an association area called the posterior parietal cortex (PPC; see Bordier et al., 2013 for a similar result). Interestingly, responses to auditory salience in the PPC were modulated by the spatial correspondence between the sounds and the visual events. This is indicative of a possible multisensory interaction. In terms of behavioural effects, the salience of both the auditory and the visual events contributed to attract the subjects' gaze. Remarkably, whether the auditory and visual events were semantically congruent or not (e.g., if the sound corresponded to the object on the screen or not) did not have any sizable effect on gaze or brain responses. This is an unexpected result because several experiments conducted under more controlled, but less realistic settings, have shown strong behavioural and brain responses to cross-modal semantic congruence (Amedi, von Kriegstein, van Atteveldt, Beauchamp, & Naumer, 2005; Beauchamp, Argall, Bodurka, Duyn, & Martin, 2004; Beauchamp, Lee, Argall, & Martin, 2004; Doehrmann & Naumer, 2008; Iordanescu et al., 2011, 2008; Laurienti et al., 2004). This constitutes a gap between laboratory findings and realistic studies, which will be important to address in the future.

So, what is the role of attention in multisensory interactions when dealing with the complexity of real-world environments? Up to this point, we can conclude that the bottom-up processes leading to automatic multisensory interactions play a limited role and are contingent on physical salience (and, by proxy, on perceptual load). These bottom-up processes, when engaged, could be based on specific multisensory mechanisms, such as feedforward convergence of unisensory inputs onto multisensory neurons and direct cortico-cortical connections between sensory brain areas. Nevertheless, other general-purpose mechanisms such as exogenous attention orienting, and alerting, can also be a vehicle for bottom-up cross-modal interactions. When physical salience of the relevant inputs is low, however, these bottom-up processes tend to wane. Top-down regulation is then necessary to select which sensory inputs engage in multisensory interaction. This top-down regulation eventually leads to the formation of multisensory representations (integration, or binding according to some authors; see Bizley, Maddox, & Lee, 2016). Multisensory attentional control sets (or attentional templates) might play a part in top-down selection in complex multisensory environments (e.g., Mast, Frings, & Spence, 2017; Matusz, Turoman, Tivadar, Retsa, & Murray, 2019). This is similar to the role that visual attentional templates play in visual selection (Folk, Remington, & Johnston, 1992). According to the neuroimaging findings discussed in this section, endogenous attention possibly acts as a selection and organisation mechanism. It does so by regulating local neural representations in sensory cortices, and by mediating the long-range communication and mutual influence across these sensory cortices. The various findings reporting attentional modulation of multisensory phenomena, such as the McGurk effect, are behavioural expressions of this top-down regulation. Beyond attention, perceptual organisation of sensory inputs in multisensory environments can be also imposed via anticipatory mechanisms based on prior knowledge, meaning, context, or expectation. These other mechanisms are discussed in the following section.

3 Prediction, Temporal Organisation, and Grouping in Complex Multisensory Scenarios

Imagine a person forcefully scratching a fork on a porcelain plate. The mere expectation of the screeching sound makes most of us feel a chilling sensation. This is an example of cross-modal anticipation. Current theoretical frameworks of human perception highlight the importance of brain mechanisms that organise and predict upcoming sensory inputs by exploiting learned statistical regularities in the environment at various temporal and spatial scales (e.g., Enns & Lleras, 2008; O'Regan, 1992; Parise, Spence, & Ernst, 2012). To paraphrase the sentiment of E. A. Maguire mentioned in the introduction of this Element, perceptual organisation and anticipation mechanisms in the brain are shaped by the regularities of the environment in which organisms have evolved. Therefore, they must play a role in real-world multisensory perception (Parise et al., 2012). This section will discuss some examples related to how multisensory perception capitalises on these regularities and their potential relevance in real-world environments.

A prominent feature of many real-world environments is that sensory inputs arrive with a regular cadence or in a predictable sequence. This is because either the originating events are intrinsically rhythmical (e.g., surfaced textures, speech, music) or because they are sampled rhythmically by our sensory systems (e.g., via respiration, saccades). According to recent proposals, there are brain mechanisms that exploit rhythmicity to anticipate upcoming sensory inputs that occur as part of predictable sequences. Phase reset and entrainment, which are physiologically related processes, are examples of such mechanisms. Phase reset happens when the excitability fluctuations of many neurons become temporarily aligned as a consequence of a perturbing event (often a sensory input). A train of such events produces the entrainment of the neural population (Lakatos et al., 2007; Schroeder & Lakatos, 2009). A variety of studies suggest that phase reset and entrainment can form the basis for prediction across sensory modalities (Kösem, Gramfort, & van Wassenhove, 2014; Romei, Gross, & Thut, 2012). We will discuss these mechanisms and provide an example of phase reset with real-world stimuli.

Another influential framework of perception that has anticipation at its core is called predictive coding (e.g., Friston, 2005, 2010). According to this proposal, perception emerges from the process of updating internal models about the environment as a function of how well they predict incoming sensory inputs. Predictive coding has been extensively used to account for multisensory perception (e.g., Arnal & Giraud, 2012; Kayser & Shams, 2015; Noppeney & Lee, 2018; Talsma, 2015; van Wassenhove et al., 2005). One of the proposals arising from these accounts is that multisensory perception involves representing the causal structure between sensory inputs via Bayesian inference based on statistical regularities of the environment (Noppeney & Lee, 2018; Rohe & Noppeney, 2015). Inferring causal structure allows grouping (or segregating) sensory inputs from different modalities according to their common (or different) causal origin. Solving this causal inference problem would result in the formation of multisensory perceptual representations. In the past, this has been called the 'problem of cross-modal pairing' (e.g., Bertelson, 1998; De Gelder & Bertelson, 2003; Welch, 1999; Welch et al., 1986) or the 'unity assumption' (e.g., Chen & Spence, 2017; Vatakis & Spence, 2007; Welch, 1999). According to many laboratory findings, one of the guiding organisational principles for pairing sensory inputs, or inferring their causal connection, is their temporal relationship (e.g., Lewald & Guski, 2003; Noppeney & Lee, 2018). Pairs of signals that begin and end around the same time are likely to originate from the same source, whereas inputs that are not correlated in time are likely to originate from different sources. Using timing in complex environments as a cue to infer multisensory objects, however, becomes challenging with large numbers of sensory inputs, given the amount of potentially alternative perceptual organisations. We will discuss some studies that have addressed how this problem might be solved.

Another important organisational principle to solve the pairing problem (or infer causal structure) is grouping sensory events according to their semantic relations (e.g., Chen & Spence, 2010; Doehrmann & Naumer, 2008; Laurienti et al., 2004; Suied, Bonneel, & Viaud-Delmon, 2009). We will consider several studies highlighting the importance of integrating semantic information across sensory modalities, the possible underlying mechanisms, and their relevance in (close to) real-world conditions.

3.1 Cross-Modal Anticipation by Phase Reset

As described above, phase reset of neural activity happens when an external event perturbs the ongoing excitability fluctuations of a population of neurons and sets them into temporary alignment. One can imagine this as the concentric ripples formed on a pond when we perturb the waters by throwing a stone. Salient stimuli produce phase reset of neural activity in sensory brain areas, and a regular train of such events produces entrainment of this neuronal activity (e.g., Lakatos, Karmos, Mehta, Ulbert, & Schroeder, 2008; Romei, Gross, & Thut, 2010; Ruzzoli & Soto-Faraco, 2014; Thut et al., 2011). This transient synchronisation of oscillatory activity produces windows of high excitability in the neural population, and it has been proposed as a mechanism of interaction between sensory modalities (Lakatos et al., 2007).

For example, intracranial recordings in animals have shown that a tactile event presented to the skin produces phase reset in the neurons of the auditory cortex (Lakatos et al., 2007). This reset in oscillations leads to a transient window of heightened excitability in the auditory cortex, making it more sensitive to incoming auditory inputs that are time-locked to the resetting (tactile) event. Other studies suggest a similar mechanism in humans (Fiebelkorn et al., 2011; Romei et al., 2012; Romei, Murray, Cappe, & Thut, 2009; Thorne, De Vos, Viola, & Debener, 2011). Some authors have extended this principle to the perception of audiovisual speech. Entrainment to the rhythmic cadence of speech, together with the predictable relationship between visual (lip dynamics) and auditory (phonemic) speech events, can form the basis for anticipation across modalities (Arnal, Doelling, & Poeppel, 2015; Arnal & Giraud, 2012; Schroeder, Lakatos, Kajikawa, Partan, & Puce, 2008). Although the concepts of phase reset and entrainment have wide appeal given the pervasive rhythmicity of some sensory inputs, evidence for their role in cross-modal interactions in real world environments is still limited. One of the few existing examples is the effect of gestures on speech processing, discussed below.

3.1.1 Cross-Modal Anticipation by Phase Reset in Real Life: the Case of Co-speech Gestures

Speakers use their hands for communication. Some of the most prevalent hand movements in speech are the so-called beat gestures. Beat gestures are flicks of the hand (and other body parts) that may not necessarily convey meaning but help emphasise their affiliate words in the discourse (McNeill, 1992). For example, politicians typically produce beat gestures during public addresses to highlight important parts of their speech. Biau et al. (Biau & Soto-Faraco, 2013; Biau, Torralba, Fuentemilla, de Diego Balaguer, & Soto-Faraco, 2015) studied how these gestures modulate speech processing in naturalistic stimuli by recording EEG from a group of participants as they watched a political address broadcasted on TV (by former Spanish president, Mr. J. L. Rodríguez Zapatero). Biau et al. (2015) found that at the onset of words affiliated with hand gestures, the EEG signal displayed an increase in phase coherence across trials compared to the same words when they appeared at other places of the discourse without hand gesture. This phase alignment was selective in the Theta band (5–6 Hz), a frequency band typical of the speech envelope (see Figure 3). The gesture-induced synchronisation of brain responses peaked at word onset but began around 100 ms before the word. This anticipatory alignment is consistent with the idea that gestures engage an oscillation-based prediction using the ongoing rhythmic structure of the speech envelope (Arnal & Giraud, 2012).

Biau et al.'s study provides a suggestive illustration of the mechanism of phase-reset at work in real-life conditions. But what functional role might this gesture-induced phase synchronisation serve in speech perception? Beat gestures often initiate in advance of their affiliate word and reach their inflexion point in synchrony with word stress. Because of this precise temporal synchronisation between gesture and speech, some authors have proposed that beat gestures play an anticipatory role during speech perception in real-life (or close to real-life) conditions (Biau, Morís Fernández, Holle, Avila, & Soto-Faraco, 2016; Biau & Soto-Faraco, 2013; Holle et al., 2012; Hubbard, Wilson, Callan, & Dapretto, 2009; Skipper, 2014; Skipper, Goldin-Meadow, Nusbaum, & Small, 2009). Confirming this idea, Biau et al. (2016) found that BOLD responses to gesture-speech stimuli in left pSTS either weakened or disappeared altogether when gestures and speech were slightly misaligned in time. Another strand of evidence for the role of gestures comes from sentence parsing experiments. Holle et al. (2012) measured ERPs to words at the end of complex sentences presented audiovisually, where the speaker could produce a gesture or not. The main finding in that study was that the amplitude of the P600 ERP component, associated with parsing syntactically challenging sentences, was reduced when gestures were present.

On the one hand, the synchronisation effect of gestures together with the exceptional sensitivity to gesture–speech alignment in brain responses suggests an anticipatory role. On the other hand, gestures seem to play a role in syntactic parsing. Based on this pattern of findings, Biau et al. (2015) suggested that during natural speech, gestures have an early attention-grabbing effect by

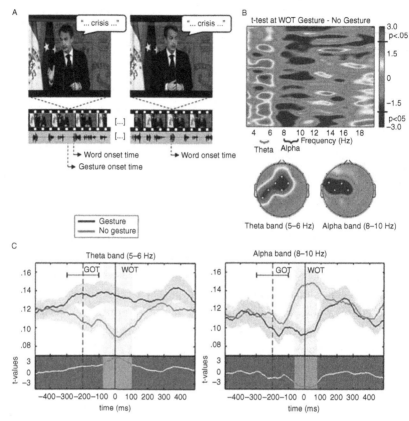

Figure 3 Top left: two side-by-side snapshots of the video clip used in Biau et al., 2015, depicting the speaker making a gesture (left) or not (right) whilst uttering the same word. Bottom left: illustration of phase reset from gestures in the delta-theta frequency, with average phase-locking, some single trials, and a circular histogram with phase distribution of trials at word onset. Top right: difference between gesture and no gesture Phase Locking Value (PLV) at word onset, across frequencies (*x*-axis) and electrodes (*y*-axis). Bottom right: topographic representation of the PLV differences above, in Theta (left) and Alpha (right), at word onset.

selectively modulating the perceptual salience of their affiliate words through cross-modal phase resetting. This attention-grabbing linguistic episode would, in turn, ease sentence parsing by reducing syntactic ambiguity. In support of this proposal, a recent ERP experiment by Biau et al. (Biau, Fromont, & Soto-Faraco, 2018), using syntactically ambiguous sentences embedded in longer discourses, observed both early word onset effects (as in Biau & Soto-Faraco, 2013; Biau et al., 2015) and P600 reduction effects (in line with Holle et al.,

2012). Results along the same lines were obtained by Dimitrova et al. (Dimitrova, Chu, Wang, Özyürek, & Hagoort, 2016). Hence, it appears that the sight of the speaker's co-speech gestures exerts an influence on the neural correlates of the affiliate speech sounds in the listener's brain. This neuroimaging evidence, however, has not yet been accompanied by sufficient evidence supporting the impact of beat gestures in behavioural measures of syntactic parsing (Biau et al., 2018) or in other aspects of speech perception (Biau, 2015). This disparity between neuroimaging and behavioural findings might have to do with ecological validity. We discuss this in the following sections.

3.1.2 The Anticipatory Effect of Gestures Is Sensitive to Real-World Conditions

As discussed in the introduction, several authors have highlighted that experiments under real-world conditions might change the outcome of tests compared to experiments done in controlled laboratory conditions (Hasson et al., 2010; Smilek et al., 2006, 2007). The mixed outcomes of beat gesture research might offer a good example of this in the multisensory domain. On the one side, neuroimaging studies have repeatedly shown fMRI and EEG effects of gestures. On the other side, the effect of beat gestures on behavioural measures of speech processing is weak when using highly naturalistic stimuli (Biau, 2015; Biau et al., 2018). These naturalistic gesture studies were conducted using long, realistic utterances (sometimes acted, sometimes spontaneous) unfolding over a time scale of seconds. The utterances contained meaningful speech stimuli in their phonological, syntactic, semantic, and pragmatic context. In contrast, other co-speech gesture studies have not been as concerned with ecological validity. For example, they used video clips where an actor uttered a list of unrelated words or where gestures were ostensibly conspicuous (Igualada, Esteve-Gibert, & Prieto, 2017; So, Sim Chen-Hui, & Low Wei-Shan, 2012). Using word lists leaves the speech stream bereft of its natural prosodic, syntactic, semantic, and pragmatic content. What is more, the impact of beat gestures on behavioural measures of speech comprehension or memory might be artificially inflated if the hand movements are far more conspicuous than they usually are in realistic contexts (e.g., So, Sim Chen-Hui, & Low Wei-Shan, 2012). In these cases, the possible subtle role that gestures could play in real-life communication might simply be altered.

Further support of the importance of using naturalistic stimuli in gesture experiments is provided by studies comparing naturally synchronised gesture-speech events to non-gesture control stimuli. For example, Hubbard et al. (2009) found that pairing speech with appropriate co-speech gestures modulates BOLD responses in classical multisensory areas (left pSTS) and in the auditory cortex (planum temporale). This is in comparison to other synchronised, but meaningless actions of the hands. In addition, the studies of Biau et al. (2016) using fMRI and Holle et al. (2012) using ERPs, both discussed above, included control conditions where the speakers' hands (performing the gestures) had been replaced with an artificial visual object (a disc) of the same size and with the same kinematics as the speaker's hand in the original videos. In both cases, under such artificial yet informationally equivalent conditions, the cross-modal effects of the visual information on speech processing simply disappeared. These findings reveal that breaches in the natural association between gestures and speech, or degradation of the linguistic context in which they occur, produce significant changes in neural responses. This could account for the mixed results in studies using highly artificial stimuli (staged gestures, while the speaker recites a list of unconnected words).

3.2 Cross-Modal Temporal Organisation in Complex Environments

Time provides critical cues to grouping and segregation of sensory events in perception. It is generally accepted that multisensory interactions between two sensory inputs are strongest when these inputs are aligned in time, and decay as temporal disparity between inputs increases (e.g., Bertelson, 1998; Lewald & Guski, 2003; Stein & Meredith, 1993; Welch, 1999; Welch et al., 1986). According to current Bayesian accounts of multisensory perception, temporal proximity can help infer causal relationships between two events (Noppeney & Lee, 2018). Moreover, temporal alignment has been proposed to be a necessary condition for automatic, bottom-up cross-modal integration (ten Oever et al., 2016). This tight relationship between temporal alignment and multisensory interaction is so widely accepted in the field, that large temporal disparities are often used as a 'no-integration' control condition in multisensory experiments. Despite the widespread agreement about the critical role of time in multisensory perception, there are challenges when trying to understand its impact in complex scenarios. One challenge is the problem of cross-modal delays; the other is the problem of pairing. Both challenges are discussed below.

The problem of cross-modal delays is as follows: because of physical and physiological delays in signal transmission outside and inside the brain, the timings of neural responses to external events do not preserve the original time relations between these events in the environment (e.g., King, 2005; Charles Spence & Squire, 2003). One reason for these delays is purely physical, as transmission speeds of different kinds of energy vary. For example, sound and light travel through the air at different speeds, something that becomes evident to the naked eye when distances are large (e.g., thunder comes after lightning). Even short distances of a few meters, however, accumulate delays that are significant in terms of brain processes (about 35 ms in a dozen meters). The second kind of cross-modal delay arises from physiology. Neural transduction and transmission processes take different amounts of time in different sensory pathways. Continuing with the example of sound and light, a sound wave arriving at the ear causes neuronal firing in the corresponding auditory cortex several tens of milliseconds earlier than light on the eye takes to produce firing of neurons in the visual cortex.

Given the critical role played by temporal synchrony in the formation of multisensory representations, the lack of temporal fidelity in neural responses can create a problem. Which pairs of events should be effectively grouped onto a perceptual object and hence produce multisensory interactions (e.g., enhancement, interference)? Researchers have proposed several mechanisms that help reconstruct the temporal organisation of sensory inputs across modalities (Fujisaki, Shimojo, Kashino, & Nishida, 2004; Morein-Zamir, Soto-Faraco, & Kingstone, 2003; Vroomen & Keetels, 2010). One of these mechanisms is called cross-modal temporal recalibration, a process that allows us to adapt to, and therefore anticipate, systematic cross-modal asynchronies. Cross-modal temporal recalibration produces shifts in the perceived temporal relation between two sensory modalities as a function of asynchronies in the immediate past (e.g., Fujisaki et al., 2004). For example, this mechanism makes us reconcile sound and sight delays when we watch a live TV broadcast from a remote location with the sound out-of-synch with the image (e.g., Navarra et al., 2005).

The cross-modal temporal recalibration mechanism has been demonstrated repeatedly under simplified settings, where only the relevant stimuli are present. But whether temporal recalibration can operate under the complexity of real-world multisensory contexts is still unknown. In real-world contexts spurious temporal coincidences between inputs can be abundant, given the many sources of stimulation present at the same time (e.g., Fujisaki et al., 2006; Roseboom, Nishida, Fujisaki, & Arnold, 2011). This is the problem of pairing inputs in time. We discuss this problem below and highlight the role of attention and ongoing neural oscillations as possible means of selection for temporal organisation in complex environments.

3.2.1 Attentional Selection Guides Temporal Organisation amidst Sensory Chaos

Laboratory work, partly reviewed in the previous section, suggests that the brain uses temporal proximity to determine which sensory inputs should be bound together to form multisensory object representations. Indeed, multisensory interactions, including cross-modal recalibration, happen only when two sensory events fall within a given, sufficiently short, temporal window (called the temporal window of integration, e.g., Spence & Squire, 2003; van Wassenhove, Grant, & Poeppel, 2007; Vroomen & Keetels, 2010). This simple heuristic strategy based on temporal proximity alone, however, might not suffice. This is because in cluttered environments temporally close, but unrelated events, occur frequently. These multiple near-simultaneous sensory events lead to competing alternative perceptual groupings. Therefore, cross-modal temporal recalibration cannot operate indiscriminately between all of the inputs present in real-life contexts. Recent findings suggest that when the temporal window of integration comprises several near-simultaneous cross-modal events, top-down processes such as endogenous attention play a fundamental role in imposing temporal organisation on the incoming inputs (Ikumi & Soto-Faraco, 2014, 2017; Ikumi et al., 2019).

A variety of studies have used the cross-modal temporal recalibration effect explained above as a proxy for whether cross-modal sensory inputs are grouped (paired) or not under complex conditions. According to the results of these studies, one selection criterion for temporal recalibration between sensory inputs embedded in complex environments is cross-modal congruence; that is, if these inputs are congruent in attributes such as spatial location or if they have been strongly associated in the past (Heron, Roach, Hanson, McGraw, & Whitaker, 2012; Roseboom, Kawabe, & Nishida, 2013; Yarrow, Roseboom, & Arnold, 2011). These studies show that stimulus-based attributes can be used as priors to organise cross-modal events in time. Other studies have shown that cross-modal organisation in time not only is based on stimulus properties, but also is exerted via endogenous top-down selection (Ikumi & Soto-Faraco, 2014, 2017; Roseboom et al., 2011). For example, Ikumi et al. (2014) presented observers with triads of sensory events consisting of a sound sandwiched between two flashes in quick succession. This arrangement leads to two mutually incompatible possible cross-modal recalibrations; that is, the sound can be recalibrated either towards the leading flash or towards the lagging flash, but not in both directions. In such cases, endogenous attention determines the recalibration direction by organising information in time (e.g., Ikumi & Soto-Faraco, 2014).

Further studies have suggested another avenue for temporal organisation. Voluntary actions can act as temporal attractors, helping organise multiple sensory inputs in time; that is, motor interactions with the environment can foster one particular perceptual grouping of sensory events therein (Arikan, van Kemenade, Straube, Harris, & Kircher, 2017; Desantis & Haggard, 2016; Ikumi

& Soto-Faraco, 2017). These results suggest that, besides exogenous processes based on stimulus-based features, endogenous processes such as attention and motor intention exert an influence in cross-modal temporal organisation. These endogenous processes might play a critical role in sensory complex environments where the salience of each individual stimulus is low. In partial support of this idea, Roseboom et al. (2011) proposed that temporally cluttered environments activate grouping mechanisms that otherwise might not operate under simpler environments. This proposal followed from the finding that temporal precision for cross-modal matching increased, rather than decreased, under sensory cluttered conditions. If confirmed, this unexpected outcome that derives from testing complex multisensory environments has interesting consequences for real-world information processing.

3.2.2 Ongoing Neural Oscillations Promote Cross-Modal Temporal Organisation

Neural oscillations refer to rhythmic fluctuations of the electrical potential in groups of neurons, which reflect excitability changes in the population.[6] These oscillations can occur spontaneously or as part of internal brain computations, and have been linked to information processing and neural communication (Buzsáki, 2006). They can be measured across large neuronal populations with noninvasive techniques, such as EEG. (Incidentally, phase reset and entrainment, discussed earlier, are ways to modulate neural oscillations by perturbation with external inputs.) Recent findings have suggested that these ongoing neural oscillations might provide a vehicle for temporal organisation. Although neuroimaging research using realistic stimuli in this topic is still lacking, there are studies using simple experimental set ups which provide initial evidence of this idea.

For example, one study shows that the amplitude of low-frequency neuronal oscillations (Alpha, 8–12 Hz, and Beta, 13–30 Hz) in sensory cortices correlates with accuracy in audiovisual temporal order judgements (Grabot, Kösem, Azizi, & van Wassenhove, 2017). Other studies show that the degree of long-range synchrony between neural oscillations in distant brain regions is linked to cross-modal temporal grouping (Hipp, Engel, & Siegel, 2011; Keil, Müller, Hartmann, & Weisz, 2014; Roa Romero, Senkowski, & Keil, 2015). Furthermore, several findings suggest that besides amplitude and long-range synchrony, the fine temporal structure conveyed in the phase of neural

---

[6] Depending on the measurement technique, the current can be measured from a population of a few localised neurons (usually invasive animal studies) or a large population of millions of neurons (scalp electrodes, in the EEG).

oscillations might provide mechanistic means for chunking the inflow of sensory information into perceptual units. Varela et al. (Varela, Toro, John, & Schwartz, 1981) were the first to test this hypothesis in the specific case of visual perception (see also Milton & Pleydell-Pearce, 2016), but some recent studies have extrapolated the idea to the case of temporal grouping across modalities (Cecere, Rees, & Romei, 2015; Ikumi, Torralba, Ruzzoli, & Soto-Faraco, 2019; Keil & Senkowski, 2017; Kösem et al., 2014).

Cross-modal grouping through oscillatory phase can be articulated in different ways. Some findings suggest that the length of the cycle of ongoing Alpha oscillations determines the size of the temporal window of integration between cross-modal inputs. That is, the time it takes for the oscillation to cycle through to a given phase bounds the window within which sensory inputs are grouped as belonging to the same event (Cecere et al., 2015; Keil & Senkowski, 2017). The hypothesis that the phase of neural oscillations sustains cross-modal temporal grouping has also received support from studies using recalibration. Kösem et al. (2014) reported that cross-modal temporal recalibration correlates with a phase-shift of oscillatory responses in sensory cortices. A recent study by Ikumi et al. (Ikumi et al., 2019) found that the phase of low-frequency neural oscillations before the presentation of a pair of cross-modal stimuli reliably predicted whether they would later be perceived as a synchronous multisensory event or as two separate single-modality ones (see Figure 4). Findings such as this, relating prestimulus neural oscillations with the perceptual outcome of multisensory interactions between upcoming events, might shed light on the brain mechanisms supporting top-down temporal organisation in complex, multisensory environments. It would be important to validate whether these oscillatory mechanisms, unveiled under simplified conditions, remain effective in more complex contexts where selection of information is critical.

3.3 Grouping by Cross-Modal Semantics

So far we have discussed grouping (or segregation) of cross-modal inputs based on their timing. Temporal proximity, however, is not the only cue leading to the formation of multisensory percepts. Several studies proposed that congruence in meaning, or semantic association, between sensory inputs can lead to grouping and eventually trigger multisensory interactions (e.g., Chen & Spence, 2010; Iordanescu et al., 2010, 2008; Laurienti et al., 2004; Mastroberardino et al., 2015; Suied et al., 2009). A striking demonstration of these semantic effects was reported by Iordanescu et al., who found that search times for images of everyday life objects (i.e., the picture of a piano) amongst distracters (e.g., pictures of a dog, a phone, and a helicopter) were faster if the subject heard

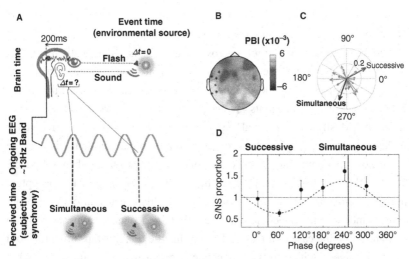

Figure 4 A. Schematic representation of the relationship between physical synchrony, asynchronies due to physiological delays, time organisation through ongoing oscillations, and phase-dependent perceptual outcome. B, C, and D are the results of Ikumi et al. (2019). B. Topographic plot representing the Phase Bifurcation Index (PBI) in the 13 Hz band at 200 ms before stimulus, in a cross-modal simultaneity judgement task. Electrodes with significant PBI are starred.
C. Individual (thin lines) and group (thick lines) phase angles for trials perceived as simultaneous and successive at the significant time-electrodes-frequency in B. D. Proportion of simultaneous responses as a function of phase (six bins) in the significant time-electrode-frequency in B. Vertical lines indicate the average phase angle for simultaneous and successive trials (from C).
Adapted from Ikumi et al. (2019).

the characteristic sound associated with the visual target object (Iordanescu et al., 2008). These findings are in line with neuroimaging evidence showing that audiovisual semantic congruence between object pictures and their characteristic sounds leads to modulation of early ERP responses such as the N1 (Molholm, Ritter, Javitt, & Foxe, 2004) and to enhanced BOLD responses in the posterior STS (Beauchamp, Lee, et al., 2004; Doehrmann & Naumer, 2008), compared to semantically incongruent picture and sound pairs. Addressing the role played by cross-modal semantics is essential to understand perception in real-life scenes because these scenes are often populated by meaningful, contextualised objects and events.

Unfortunately, the mechanisms underlying cross-modal semantic interactions in perception are controversial. Some studies, like the one by Iordanescu et al. (2008) mentioned earlier, have suggested that semantic interactions across modalities could happen automatically, before attentional selection. Nevertheless, not all findings are consistent with this suggestion. As we discussed in the context of bottom-up cross-modal effects, a diagnostic feature for automaticity is whether the interaction of interest occurs for task-irrelevant, unattended objects. Yet, the evidence for cross-modal semantic interactions between task-irrelevant inputs is weak, especially when considering real-life scenarios (Mastroberardino et al., 2015; Nardo et al., 2014). An alternative (or perhaps complementary) account for cross-modal semantic interactions is the well-known phenomenon of conceptual or semantic priming (Chen & Spence, 2010, 2011; Schneider, Engel, & Debener, 2008). According to conceptual priming, semantic content in one sensory modality creates an expectation in another modality by association or repetition of concepts, thereby speeding up recognition in the case of a match. These semantic relationships are built from prior experience with correlations between cross-modal events, such as the association between the sound of barking and the sight of a dog (e.g., Beierholm, Quartz, & Shams, 2009; Parise et al., 2012; Parise & Spence, 2009). Several results reveal effects of semantic priming across modalities, and how these effects have different time courses as a function of the format of the priming information (e.g., a spoken word, or the characteristic sound associated to a given visual object; Chen & Spence, 2013, 2018a, 2018b).

Another possible basis for (at least some) cross-modal semantic interactions are *cross-modal correspondences*. Cross-modal correspondences refer to mappings between sensory properties in different modalities that are seemingly arbitrary yet turn out to be widely shared amongst people. These mappings, albeit surprising, could have an origin in actual environmental correlations (Parise, Knorre, & Ernst, 2014). One oft-studied cross-modal correspondence would be the link between the pitch of sounds and elevation in space; high-pitched sounds are associated with higher spatial locations (see Spence, 2011 for a review).

Even if the core mechanism for cross-modal semantic interactions might not differ much from other forms of perceptual and conceptual priming happening within a modality, cross-modal priming may carry some added value in comparison to the unisensory case (e.g., Laurienti et al., 2004; Pesquita et al., 2013). For example, in visual priming, seeing the image of a dog will facilitate the recognition of other subsequent images of dogs based on reactivating the same concept (e.g., Wiggs & Martin, 1998). Likewise, in the cross-modal case, the sound of a barking dog facilitates visual recognition of dogs by conceptual repetition, but it might also generate additional expectations about other visual attributes, such as the size of the animal or its emotional state. Pesquita et al. (2013) addressed this question using visuo-haptic interactions (see also Reales

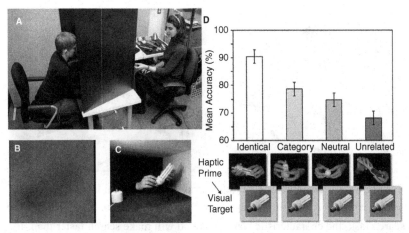

Figure 5 A. Setup in Pesquita et al.'s study 2013. Participants watched a progressively deblurred picture of an object (see B) to be identified, whilst they explored an object with the hands (see C). In different conditions, the hand-held prime object could be physically identical, same category, or unrelated to the visual target as shown in the illustrations below the accuracy plot (see D; error bars indicate s.e.m.).

& Ballesteros, 1999). In Pesquita et al.'s study participants were asked to spot everyday objects in blurred pictures while haptically exploring an actual physical object with their hands. As predicted by classic conceptual priming, recognition was more efficient when the haptic prime was of the same category as the blurred visual target (e.g., recognising the picture of a stapler while manually examining a stapler), than when of a different category. The interesting result was that the priming effect was stronger if the haptic prime and visual target objects were physically identical compared to when they were different tokens of the same type of object (see Figure 5). This finding denotes that above and beyond purely conceptual facilitation, there was some priming between structural properties (e.g., shape, texture) that transferred across sensory modalities.

The experiments on cross-modal semantics discussed above suggest that high-level congruence relationships amongst real objects (or pictures thereof) have an impact on behaviour. Nevertheless, we hasten to remind the reader that hitherto, most of them used stereotyped and artificial scenarios that lacked a meaningful context. Knoeferle et al. (Knoeferle, Knoeferle, Velasco, & Spence, 2016) took one step into generalising these protocols to everyday contexts. In their study, sounds (and jingles) associated with commercial products were found to modulate visual search times in displays

Figure 6 Left: example of a stimulus array used in typical laboratory search tasks that address cross-modal semantic effects. If the *stapler* is the target of the search task, the characteristic stapling sound will make search faster than, for example, the sound of a dog barking. Right: naturalistic image containing a stapler. Visual complexity and clutter lower the visibility of the target object, yet the semantics in the scene considerably constrain the search space by prioritising probable locations (e.g., table top). Whether previous laboratory-based effects of cross-modal semantic facilitation apply in these realistic conditions is not known.

recreating supermarket shelves. In the future, it will be important to go beyond isolated objects into more real-life–like scenarios where cross-modal semantic interactions are studied in meaningful, structured, and dynamical contexts (see Peelen & Kastner, 2014; Wu, Wick, & Pomplun, 2014 for examples in visual-only scenarios). For instance, searching for an object in regular arrays, as typically used in laboratory tasks, is very different than searching for an object in irregular but structured, naturalistic scenes. Such natural scenarios provide meaningful structure and make prior experience useful. Imagine searching for your cat in the living room; you would not expect to find the cat hovering in mid-air, next to a floating grand piano. Many laboratory tasks require just that (see Figure 6). In these laboratory experiments, the image of a (target) cat can appear within a set of decontextualised objects, arranged in a regular circle, against a solid textureless background. Multisensory studies including rich, meaningful, everyday contexts are very few (see Kvasova & Soto-Faraco, 2019, for a recent example). Surprisingly, the significant cross-modal semantic effects found in idealised laboratory settings have not always been observed in more realistic conditions (e.g., Nardo et al., 2014). Future studies will have to close this gap by generalising cross-modal semantic effects found using controlled protocols to naturalistic contexts.

4 The Role of Conflict in Multisensory Interactions

A report by Transport for London,[7] published before the 2012 Olympics, warned that one of the reasons tourists are more likely to be involved in accidents is that 'visitors assume traffic will come from the wrong direction'. It is well-known that visitors to the UK must refrain from the automatic routine of checking the left side of the road and take the appropriate action of checking right-incoming traffic first. This is a clear case of conflict between alternative courses of action. In more general terms, cognitive conflict arises upon 'the simultaneous activation of incompatible and competing representations' (Botvinick, Cohen, & Carter, 2004). It happens when people must inhibit a routine response and plan a non-routine action, like in the street-crossing example (i.e., stimulus–response conflict), or when sensory information supports alternative and incompatible perceptual interpretations (i.e., stimulus–stimulus conflict).

The detection of conflict triggers cognitive control, meaning that cognitive resources are recruited to resolve the inconsistency (e.g., Botvinick, Braver, Barch, Carter, & Cohen, 2001; Botvinick, Cohen, & Carter, 2004). There are well-established laboratory protocols that are used to test conflict under controlled conditions. These include the Stroop task (MacLeod, 1991; Stroop, 1935), the Flanker task (Eriksen & Eriksen, 1974), and the Simon task (Simon & Small Jr, 1969). For example, in the Simon task, participants must make rapid discrimination responses by pressing a button with either their left or right hand regarding the colour of a visual stimulus, which can appear on the left or right on a computer monitor. Responses are faster (and more accurate) if stimulus and response sides match than if they do not, even if the stimulus location (left/right on the computer screen) is completely task irrelevant. The interpretation is that the appearance of the stimulus triggers an involuntary tendency to act upon its location, which can be incompatible with the correct response (to colour, in the example). Experiments using conflict protocols such as these have provided grounding evidence for current theories about conflict monitoring and the associated brain correlates, which classically include the anterior cingulate cortex (ACC) and the dorso-lateral prefrontal cortex (DLPFC) (Botvinick, 2007; Botvinick et al., 2001, 2004; Clayton, Yeung, & Cohen Kadosh, 2015; Roberts & Hall, 2008; Shenhav, Botvinick, & Cohen, 2013).

The interplay between conflict and multisensory interaction processes in the context of real-world scenarios can raise relevant questions. It is surprising that the research traditions of cognitive conflict and multisensory processing have followed mostly separate paths. For example, one question refers to stimulus–

---

[7] http://content.tfl.gov.uk/visitor-pedestrian-safety-final-report.pdf

response conflict when events in various modalities can trigger involuntary responses, as often occurs in real-world scenarios. A second question refers to the role of the conflict-processing mechanisms when different sensory modalities are in disagreement about a stimulus (called inter-sensory conflict). Answering this second question is important not only to understand how our perceptual system solves the causal inference (or pairing) problem discussed in the previous section, but also because inter-sensory conflict has been extensively used in the laboratory as a proxy to study multisensory interactions. What does this research tell us about real-world perception, where multisensory objects are characterised by congruent instead of conflicting cues?

A few recent studies have started to unveil possible connections between multisensory perception and conflict mechanisms (e.g., Alsius, Paré, & Munhall, 2018; Castro, Soto-Faraco, Morís Fernández, & Ruzzoli, 2018; Morís Fernández et al., 2017, 2018, 2015; Ruzzoli & Soto-Faraco, 2017). Below we outline initial findings on the role of conflict in two multisensory cases: sensory-motor conflict in multisensory scenarios and in inter-sensory conflict during audiovisual speech perception.

4.1 Sensory-Motor Conflict in Cross-Modal Scenarios

In the Simon task, described earlier, the location of visual events can trigger automatic reactions that can interfere with the intended behaviour. In real-world multisensory environments, these involuntary reactions to the location of a stimulus can be summoned by events in different sensory modalities. One could initially think of stimulus–response conflict in these multisensory contexts just like one would treat conflict in the unisensory case, only that sometimes it happens in response to a sensory event in one modality, and at other times in response to a different modality. According to recent findings, however, things are not as straightforward as that. A source of confusion in the multisensory case is that different modalities code spatial location according to different frames of reference. In vision and audition, the dominant reference frame is outside the body (i.e., external). Conversely, in touch, the relevant frame of reference is internal (i.e., anatomical). What, then, is the dominant frame of reference when events from various modalities can activate involuntary responses?

Until very recently studies addressing spatial compatibility effects in the Simon task have not provided an answer to this question because they have used just one stimulus modality at a time; audition (e.g., Röder, Kusmierek, Spence, & Schicke, 2007; Roswarski & Proctor, 2000; Simon, Hinrichs, & Craft, 1970; Wallace, 1972), vision (e.g., Riggio, de Gonzaga Gawryszewski, &

Umilta, 1986; Wallace, 1972), or touch (e.g., Hasbroucq & Guiard, 1991; Medina, McCloskey, Coslett, & Rapp, 2014). Spatial compatibility effects found in these studies are in line with the dominant reference frame of each sensory modality. Recent studies, however, show that these outcomes can change in significant ways just by mixing events from different modalities.

Ruzzoli & Soto-Faraco (2017) conducted various experiments using the classic Simon task, only that visual and tactile events were mixed unpredictably. The results showed that under these conditions, spatial-compatibility effects disappeared in vision, but not in touch. This outcome was unexpected because the visual Simon effect is a very robust phenomenon (Hommel, 2011; Proctor & Lu, 1999) and because the visual spatial frame of reference often overrides that of touch in other spatial tasks (Azañón & Soto-Faraco, 2008; Yamamoto & Kitazawa, 2001). The vanishing of the visual Simon effect in visuo-tactile contexts was attributed to having to handle various frames of reference concurrently (in visual perception the frame of reference is external, and in touch it is anatomical). Indeed, when mixing visual and auditory events, which both have external reference frames, spatial-compatibility occurred normally in either modality. A subsequent EEG study by Castro et al. (2018) evaluated the neural correlates of spatial compatibility in single-modality versus mixed-modality (vision, touch) Simon tasks through three proxies: the P300 delay in ERP responses, the lateralised readiness potential (LRP), and the EEG fronto-medial Theta power. Supporting Ruzzoli & Soto-Faraco's (2017) results, neural correlates of spatial-incompatibility showed up in single-modality visual contexts, but they disappeared from vision (or weakened to a non-significant extent) when visual trials were intermingled with tactile trials.

The results discussed above reveal that evidence about stimulus–response conflict gathered from single-modality experiments could not anticipate the outcome in mixed-modality contexts, with the latter being more representative of real-world scenarios. The initial interpretation of these findings was that various spatial reference frames cannot be used simultaneously to control behaviour. Therefore, when only one reference frame is relevant for behaviour (single-modality context) then it can be prepared for in advance. But when an environment contains events in different modalities, their associated frames of reference enter in competition to prepare for action. Because of this competition, the relevant frame of reference may vary considerably as a function of the sensory context and task demands. In some multisensory contexts, like the mixed-modality Simon experiments discussed here, the anatomical reference frame regulates behaviour while the external reference frame shuts down, or nearly so (Castro et al., 2018; Ruzzoli & Soto-Faraco, 2017). Yet, in other contexts and tasks, an external reference frame may prevail over the anatomical one, as shown by the crossed-hands effects in touch (e.g., Azañón & Soto-Faraco, 2008; Heed, Buchholz, Engel, & Röder, 2015; Medina et al., 2014; Yamamoto & Kitazawa, 2001). This account of competing frames of reference can also explain earlier findings in single-modality experiments, where the visual Simon effect was occasionally eliminated by mixing reference frames within vision (e.g., Hommel, 1993; Ladavas & Moscovitch, 1984; Lamberts, Tavernier, & d'Ydewalle, 1992; Roswarski & Proctor, 2000; Stoffer, 1991; Umiltà & Liotti, 1987).

In sum, the dominant reference frame to encode the location of sensory events might be more flexible than had been previously thought, based on single-modality experiments. Although the theoretical implications outlined above are still tentative (see Castro et al., 2018), the empirical findings can have a practical impact on interface design. For example, we can expect that using haptic alerts on the body, such as those on cell phones, smart watches, or in-car tactile warnings (e.g., Ho, Reed, & Spence, 2006; Ho, Tan, & Spence, 2005; Scott & Gray, 2008; Spence & Ho, 2008), might induce a momentary shutdown of the external reference frame, with detrimental consequences (slower reactions, more errors) for emergency reactions in visual-spatial tasks such as driving.

4.2 Stimulus–Stimulus Conflict in Cross-Modal Events

Although the case of conflict between stimulus and response is thought to have a special status, the core conceptual framework of conflict processing applies to the case of conflict between two stimuli (Botvinick et al., 2001; Clayton et al., 2015; Jiang, Zhang, & Van Gaal, 2015; Morís Fernández et al., 2017, 2018; Weissman, Giesbrecht, Song, Mangun, & Woldorff, 2003). In fact, countless real-world examples of stimulus–stimulus conflict can be found in advertisement, where perceptual incongruence is often used as a device to summon the viewer's attention by generating surprise[8]. This creative resource, inherited from the surrealist artistic movement, has been called 'divergence' in marketing science (Smith, MacKenzie, Yang, Buchholz, & Darley, 2007).

Interestingly, conflict between sensory inputs (e.g., stimulus–stimulus conflict) is extensively used as a method to study multisensory processes. For instance, all cross-modal illusions are based on conflict between sensory cues. To name a few famous cases, the ventriloquist[9] illusion arises from audiovisual

---

[8] Here is a link to one of the commercials from a Taco Bell advertising campaign in the 1990s, where the strategy of conflict was famously used: https://youtu.be/ygW0VV_kotI

[9] The ventriloquist effect is a perceptual illusion regarding the mislocalisation of the source of a sound towards the position of a simultaneously occurring visual event. The name of the illusion makes reference to the stage performance, but the effect can be reproduced in the laboratory using

spatial conflict (Bertelson, 1998), the McGurk illusion stems from phonemic conflict between speech sounds and mouth gestures (McGurk & MacDonald, 1976), and the rubber hand illusion[10] from visuo-proprioceptive conflict (Botvinick & Cohen, 1998). In addition to multisensory illusions, conflict is the method of choice in experiments addressing Bayesian models of multi-sensory integration. According to the Bayesian approach, humans weigh inputs (cues) from the various sensory modalities as a function of their reliabilities. The predictions of Bayesian models are often evaluated against the empirical results of inter-sensory conflict so that the relative weights given to each sensory modality can be revealed (e.g., Alais & Burr, 2004; Ernst & Banks, 2002).

Because of the extensive use of conflict in multisensory research, it is perhaps surprising that the interplay between conflict and multisensory processes has rarely been addressed in the literature. As pointed out in Morís-Fernández et al. (2017, 2015), activity in conflict-related brain areas (such as the ACC) is regularly found in cross-modal neuroimaging studies, albeit rarely discussed (Gau & Noppeney, 2016; Miller & D'esposito, 2005; Noppeney, Josephs, Hocking, Price, & Friston, 2008; Ojanen et al., 2005; Pekkola et al., 2006; Szycik, Jansma, & Münte, 2009). Next we provide an example of how considering the interplay between conflict and multisensory processes can lead to new insights.

4.2.1 Multisensory Interactions As Conflict Resolution

The McGurk effect[11] is a textbook example of multisensory integration. This illusion arises from phonemic conflict (whether consciously registered or not) between speech sounds and the sight of a speaker's lip movements (e.g., Andersen, Tiippana, & Sams, 2004; Bernstein, Auer, Wagner, & Ponton, 2008; Hasson, Skipper, Nusbaum, & Small, 2007; Skipper, Van Wassenhove, Nusbaum, & Small, 2007; Soto-Faraco, Navarra, & Alsius, 2004; Tiippana, 2014; van Wassenhove et al., 2007). For example, the sound of the syllable 'BA' dubbed on a speaker's face mouthing the syllable 'GA' will be heard as 'DA' (see Figure 1, in Section 2, for a more detailed description). Despite its tremendous popularity as a model to study multisensory integration in the laboratory and the obvious fact that the McGurk effect involves stimulus–stimulus conflict, there has been surprisingly little effort to frame this illusion within the conflict processing theory. This is perhaps even more remarkable

---

a variety of different stimuli such as speech, everyday objects, or just beeps and flashes (Connor, 2000). A demonstration can be found at: https://youtu.be/NrAtw-VBYmY

[10] An explanation of the rubber hand illusion can be found at: https://youtu.be/TCQbygjG0RU

[11] A professionally produced example can be found in BBC Two's 2010 piece on the McGurk illusion: https://youtu.be/G-lN8vWm3m0

given that several fMRI studies using McGurk stimuli have in fact observed BOLD responses in classic conflict brain areas, such as the ACC (Benoit, Raij, Lin, Jääskeläinen, & Stufflebeam, 2010; Bernstein, Lu, & Jiang, 2008; Malfait et al., 2014) and areas sensitive to audiovisual speech mismatch such as the inferior frontal gyrus (IFG) (Matchin, Groulx, & Hickok, 2014).

Recently, Morís-Fernández et al. (2017) addressed the role of conflict mechanisms in the McGurk illusion using fMRI. Morís-Fernandez et al. measured brain activity in response to audiovisually presented syllables in four conditions. Two of the conditions involved identical stimulation (McGurk syllables) but were sorted as a function of the subject's perception. Either the illusion was experienced (integration outcome) or else the veridical sound was perceived (no integration). The other two conditions involved either normal audiovisual matching syllables (congruent syllables leading to integration; /BA/ sound with /BA/ lips), or audiovisually mismatched syllables that were not conducive to integration (the sound /BA/ was dubbed with the backward video of /BA/ lips). Hence, the authors could gauge the effects of conflict with and without perceptual integration (illusorily perceived vs. non-illusory McGurk trials). The results were clear (see Figure 7); regardless of the perceptual outcome (perception of the McGurk illusion or not), all kinds of inter-sensory conflict activated conflict areas (e.g., ACC) as well as specific brain regions typically responsive to audiovisual mismatch in speech (e.g., IFG). In a further study, using EEG, Morís-Fernández et al. (2018) confirmed this finding, showing that McGurk events, just like Stroop stimuli, induced an increase in frontro-central Theta power, a well-known electrophysiological response to conflict (see Figure 7).

An interpretation of Morís-Fernández et al.'s (2017, 2018, 2015) findings, described above, is that McGurk stimuli trigger an initial detection of conflict (expressed in the ACC response) upon the attempt to integrate mismatching audiovisual cues. Subsequently, resources to resolve this conflict would be recruited through the engagement of other areas (such as the IFG and the PC). This brain network could either succeed at resolving the audiovisual mismatch by integrating the cues into a single (but illusory) percept, or else fail, leading to lack of integration (not experiencing the illusion). An independent study by Roa-Romero et al. (2015) suggested a similar conflict detection and resolution two-stage account, based on EEG responses to McGurk stimuli in the Beta band.

Do these findings mean then that inter-sensory conflict, such as the McGurk illusion, involves a different set of brain areas than the processing of cross-modally congruent events, such as naturalistic (audiovisually matching) speech? Not necessarily. The framework outlined above might extend beyond

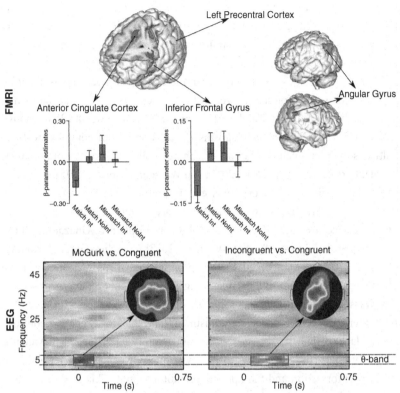

Figure 7 The results of two separate experiments. Above: BOLD activity resulting from whole-brain analysis of the interaction effect resulting from the contrast McGurk syllables perceived as illusory (integrated) versus equivalent McGurk syllables when perceived as veridical (not integrated), compared to audiovisually perfectly matched (integrated) versus completely mismatched (not integrated) syllables (adapted from Morís-Fernández et al., 2015). Below: two side-by-side time-frequency plots with the Theta frequency band highlighted, showing increases in Theta power with respect to the moment of sound onset in audiovisually mismatched syllables (left) and McGurk syllables (right), with respect to an audiovisually congruent condition. Insets show topographic plots of the selected time and frequency (Theta) effect highlighted in the main graph (adapted from Morís-Fernández et al., 2018).

the relatively artificial setting of the McGurk illusion to real-life audiovisual speech perception. Conflict detection processes play a monitoring role in naturalistic speech perception, but because audiovisual mismatch is rare in real-life speech, the need to engage control mechanisms (e.g., resolve conflicts) seldom arises. This is also what happens in other domains, such as motor control, perceptual integration, and even navigation; conflict monitoring is an ongoing process (i.e., running in the background) which only occasionally triggers a call for high-cost strategies of executive control (Shenhav, Botvinick, & Cohen, 2013).

We further speculate that the proposed role of conflict mechanisms in audiovisual speech perception aligns well with the predictive coding accounts discussed earlier (Arnal & Giraud, 2012; Skipper et al., 2007; van Wassenhove et al., 2005). Anticipatory mechanisms act on a variety of complex, real-life multisensory phenomena including speech perception (Schroeder et al., 2008; Stekelenburg & Vroomen, 2007, 2012; van Wassenhove et al., 2005). In speech perception, visible articulatory cues enable prediction regarding the timing (Arnal et al., 2015) and phonological category of the corresponding speech sounds (Chandrasekaran, Trubanova, Stillittano, Caplier, & Ghazanfar, 2009; Sánchez-García, Enns, & Soto-Faraco, 2013; Sánchez-García, Kandel, Savariaux, & Soto-Faraco, 2018). We propose that disparities between the visually based prediction and the upcoming auditory input produce error signals (van Wassenhove et al., 2005). When the disparity (and hence error signal) is small, there will be little need for adjustment (and thus for executive control). Instead, large disparities between visual and auditory cues, such as in McGurk stimuli, produce correspondingly large deviations between the prediction based on visual information and the upcoming auditory input. This leads to a large error signal in terms of the predictive coding framework (e.g., Noppeney & Lee, 2018; van Wassenhove et al., 2005), which in turn triggers a conflict signal and the ensuing recruitment of control mechanisms to resolve the perceptual inconsistency.

5 Conclusions

Multisensory research originally held the promise of ecological validity; that is, a better understanding of perception amidst the sensory complexity that characterises our everyday life environments (e.g., De Gelder & Bertelson, 2003; Driver & Spence, 1998; Stein & Meredith, 1993). To some extent this promise has been fulfilled. The debates that have animated the field throughout the years have led to a better understanding (or at least intuition) of the behavioural, physiological, and computational principles that govern multisensory interactions. Notwithstanding these efforts, the impact that multisensory interactions have in information processing during our everyday life perception is still largely unknown. For example, well-controlled laboratory experiments using illusions such as the ventriloquist or the McGurk effects resulted in the idea that multisensory integration is automatic and unavoidable (e.g., Bertelson &

Aschersleben, 1998; Bertelson et al., 2000; Soto-Faraco et al., 2004). If this were completely true, however, real-world scenarios cluttered with myriad unconnected sensory inputs should lead to constant episodes of spurious *ventriloquisation* between unrelated events. Dubbed movies would be utterly confusing because of the unwanted intrusion of illusory sounds due to McGurk illusions. Yet, this does not seem to correspond to our everyday life experience. Why?

An answer to this question is emerging from the study of multisensory interactions in the context of other information processing mechanisms such as attention, prediction, temporal grouping, and conflict. Thanks to the interplay between multisensory processes and these other mechanisms, our brains can harness the benefits of multisensory integration whilst efficiently preventing perceptual distortion due to fortuitous coincidences of unrelated sensory inputs in crowded scenarios. In this Element, we have highlighted studies that uncover this interplay by addressing the generalisation of multisensory interactions, often studied in isolation, in contexts where they are intertwined with other mechanisms. This research strategy will shed light on how multisensory perception works in real-world conditions. The findings reviewed here are partial, and representative of real-world situations to a varying, rather modest, degree. But even this modest approximation already reveals some important conclusions.

5.1 Attention and Multisensory Interactions in Real-World Contexts

Selection mechanisms, needed for perceptual processing in real-world complex environments, affect multisensory interaction in profound ways. This is especially the case in situations of high perceptual load, where no single event stands out amongst the others. We have reviewed examples of this attention mediation showing that the behavioural and neural outcomes of integration weaken when attention is pulled away from the to-be-integrated inputs (e.g., Alsius et al., 2014, 2005; Alsius et al., 2007; Fairhall & Macaluso, 2009; Morís Fernández et al., 2015; Senkowski et al., 2008; Tiippana et al., 2004). In cases where sensory information exceeds processing capacity, access to the integration machinery is granted only through top-down selection of the relevant sensory inputs. Selection before integration, however, is not a rule written in stone. Sometimes, multisensory interactions can be 'guided' by one unique, salient event in one of the modalities, which acts as an anchor for concurrent events in other modalities in cluttered environments (Maddox et al., 2015; Van Der Burg et al., 2008). Cross-modal cueing in space and time could be a behavioural expression of this bottom-up mechanism (Andersen & Mamassian, 2008; Lippert et al., 2007; Pérez-Bellido et al., 2013). Cross-modal phase reset (e.g., Lakatos et al., 2007; Schroeder & Lakatos, 2009) and attention-spreading (Busse et al., 2005; Talsma et al., 2010) are possible physiological mechanisms for these interactions, but their role in real-life contexts is still unknown. Other proposals of bottom-up cross-modal integration mechanisms might be based on direct (feedforward) convergence of sensory inputs. This early convergence is expressed in short-latency, sensory-level multisensory responses (Andersen & Mamassian, 2008; Foxe et al., 2000; Foxe & Schroeder, 2005; Jaekl et al., 2014; Nelken, Bizley, Shamma, & Wang, 2014; Pérez-Bellido et al., 2013).

5.2 Prediction, Temporal Organisation, and Grouping in Real-World Multisensory Environments

This Element has also made a point about the importance of timing and sensory prediction in real-life multisensory processing. Our everyday life environments are sensorially complex but structured and predictable in many ways. Structure can be extracted from a variety of domains (e.g., time, space, semantic associations) and at a variety of scales (milliseconds to years, millimetres to thousands of kilometres, simple semantic associations to cultural concepts). Predictive mechanisms that exploit these regularities are increasingly recognised in many areas of perception, including multisensory processing (e.g., Noppeney & Lee, 2018, for a recent proposal). One example is cross-modal prediction based on the temporal regularity of speech. Predictive coding uses the rhythmic envelope of speech to anticipate the timing of sounds, and visual cues arising from orofacial speech gestures are used to anticipate phonological categories in the acoustic input (Arnal et al., 2015; Arnal & Giraud, 2012; van Wassenhove et al., 2005). Prediction during perceptual processing has been related to physiological mechanisms including phase reset and entrainment. Whilst well-controlled laboratory research has shown that these physiological mechanisms can lead to cross-modal interaction (e.g., Lakatos et al., 2007; Schroeder & Lakatos, 2009), research on hand gestures has provided some validation of this hypothesis using real-life stimuli (Biau et al., 2015).

Timing has been highlighted as an organisational principle in multisensory perception, but how this temporal organisation might help extract multisensory objects from the complexity of real-world environments is still not fully understood (e.g., Ikumi & Soto-Faraco, 2014, 2017). Spatial proximity, learned associations, selective attention, and grouping by action may play a role. Ongoing neural oscillations have been proposed as a relevant physiological mechanism in temporal organisation of cross-modal inputs (e.g., Ikumi et al.,

2019; Kösem et al., 2014), but their role in complex environments is unknown. Finally, other forms of anticipation involve capitalising upon learned cross-modal semantic associations. Most real-life environments are characterised by the presence of objects interrelated in a structured, meaningful way. Thus common semantic associations can form the basis of multisensory interactions that may be captured more effectively by studies using realistic objects and scenes (e.g., Doehrmann & Naumer, 2008; Iordanescu et al., 2011, 2008). The underlying mechanism of these cross-modal semantic effects, however, is yet to be agreed upon (Chen & Spence, 2011). Remarkably, significant cross-modal semantic effects obtained with artificial displays seem to be difficult to generalise under real-life scenarios, but more research is clearly needed in this area (Nardo et al., 2014).

5.3 Conflict and Multisensory Interactions

The study of how conflict is detected and resolved has a long tradition in cognitive neuroscience (e.g., Botvinick et al., 2001, 2004). The impact of conflict mechanisms in multisensory processing, however, has been largely neglected. Real-world conditions provide the grounds for interplay between conflict and multisensory processes. This Element has highlighted two examples of such interplay and the possible conclusions to be derived from them.

First, the coordination of spatial reference frames in sensorimotor conflict tasks, when events in various modalities are at play, may deviate in important ways with respect to the more typically studied single-modality case. Because different modalities encode events in different spatial reference frames, spatial information must be orchestrated to generate representations under a common coordinate system, ready to plan actions. Interestingly, not many studies had addressed stimulus–response spatial conflict in multisensory scenarios (Castro et al., 2018; Ruzzoli & Soto-Faraco, 2017). It seems that, although spatial codes are activated automatically (creating spatial compatibility effects such as the Simon effect), only one spatial reference frame can be used at a time to refer to these spatial codes. We proposed that the dominant reference frame arises from a competition between the various potential reference frames available. The outcome of this competition depends on the sensory modalities involved, the task at hand, and internal goals. It remains to be seen which reference frames are important in which real-life environments, so that information processing can be made most efficient. For example, the reference frame relevant whilst driving a vehicle can be determined by sudden acoustic or tactile warning signals, with potentially important consequences.

Second, we have considered the interplay between multisensory processes and inter-sensory conflict. Cross-modal research has often resorted to inter-sensory conflict, and its use dates back to the studies of Viktor Urbantschitsch about sound localisation, nearly 140 years ago (Urbantschitsch, 1880). Yet, the role of conflict processing mechanisms in these inter-sensory conflict situations has been largely neglected. We have highlighted that mismatch between cross-modal inputs triggers general-purpose conflict processing machinery. This finding is relevant not only because many findings in multisensory perception are based on inter-sensory conflict tasks, but because it may reveal a role for inter-sensory conflict in the perception of real-world naturalistic stimuli. To illustrate this point, we have put the focus on the McGurk effect, a popular illusion used as a model for multisensory integration (Alsius et al., 2018). We have highlighted that one must exert caution when generalising findings arising from inter-sensory conflict paradigms, because mismatch between sensory cues engages conflict-related machinery. We have also proposed that one possible framework to situate inter-sensory conflict and multisensory processing of natural stimuli on a common ground is predictive coding (Morís Fernández et al., 2017, 2018, 2015). Under the framework of predictive coding, one can consider multisensory interactions as a predictive process whereby one sensory modality helps narrow down the possible interpretations of another (an account also called analysis by synthesis). Large error signals happen when predictions built from one modality grossly mismatch the actual input on another modality. In terms of conflict processing, these large error signals could lead to conflict detection in an ongoing (and domain-general) conflict monitoring process. Under naturalistic circumstances, the conflict monitoring process would run in the background but only occasionally invoke control for conflict resolution (upon large disparity between prediction and input).

5.4 Concluding Remarks

Understanding how multisensory interactions found in the laboratory play out in real-world situations is a fascinating challenge. Nonetheless, this endeavour will necessarily face complications. This Element has attempted to exemplify the challenge by highlighting a few illustrative cases. One of the difficulties pointed out is to strike the right balance between experimental control and realism. A second complication is that the interplay of multisensory interactions with other cognitive processes (such as attention, prediction, grouping, and conflict) can alter the expression of known multisensory phenomena in dramatic ways. A possible strategy to face this challenge is to adopt incremental steps using 'naturalistic laboratory research'. Advancing in this research program should help clarify which multisensory effects have a significant impact in our everyday life contexts and which others are true in the laboratory but simply negligible in real-life. Ultimately, we (researchers) should help other communities use cross-modal interactions to, for example, come up with better designs, improve road safety, foster cross-modal plasticity to overcome sensory loss, or, referring to one of the opening examples, simply to make meals more enjoyable.

List of Acronyms

EEG   Electroencephalography
fMRI   Functional Magnetic Resonance Imaging
BOLD   Blood Oxygen Level-Dependent signal
MEG   Magnetoencephalography
ERP   Event-Related Potential

References

Alais, D., & Burr, D. (2004). The ventriloquist effect results from near-optimal bimodal integration. *Current Biology, 14*(3), 257–62.

Alsius, A., Möttönen, R., Sams, M. E., Soto-Faraco, S., & Tiippana, K. (2014). Effect of attentional load on audiovisual speech perception: evidence from ERPs. *Frontiers in Psychology, 5*(JUL). https://doi.org/10.3389/fpsyg.2014.00727

Alsius, A., Navarra, J., Campbell, R., & Soto-Faraco, S. (2005). Audiovisual integration of speech falters under high attention demands. *Current Biology, 15*(9), 839–43. https://doi.org/10.1016/j.cub.2005.03.046

Alsius, A., Navarra, J., & Soto-Faraco, S. (2007). Attention to touch weakens audiovisual speech integration. *Experimental Brain Research, 183*(3), 399–404. https://doi.org/10.1007/s00221-007-1110-1

Alsius, A., Paré, M., & Munhall, K. G. (2018). Forty years after hearing lips and seeing voices: the McGurk effect revisited. *Multisensory Research, 31*(1–2), 111–44. https://doi.org/10.1163/22134808–00002565

Alsius, A., & Soto-Faraco, S. (2011). Searching for audiovisual correspondence in multiple speaker scenarios. *Experimental Brain Research, 213*(2–3). https://doi.org/10.1007/s00221-011–2624–0

Amedi, A., von Kriegstein, K., van Atteveldt, N. M., Beauchamp, M. S., & Naumer, M. J. (2005). Functional imaging of human crossmodal identification and object recognition. *Experimental Brain Research, 166*(3–4), 559–71. https://doi.org/10.1007/s00221-005–2396–5

Andersen, T. S., & Mamassian, P. (2008). Audiovisual integration of stimulus transients. *Vision Research, 48*(25), 2537–44. https://doi.org/10.1016/J.VISRES.2008.08.018

Andersen, T. S., Tiippana, K., Laarni, J., Kojo, I., & Sams, M. (2009). The role of visual spatial attention in audiovisual speech perception. *Speech Communication, 51*(2), 184–93. https://doi.org/10.1016/J.SPECOM.2008.07.004

Andersen, T. S., Tiippana, K., & Sams, M. (2004). Factors influencing audiovisual fission and fusion illusions. *Cognitive Brain Research, 21*(3), 301–8.

Arikan, B. E., van Kemenade, B. M., Straube, B., Harris, L. R., & Kircher, T. (2017). Voluntary and involuntary movements widen the window of subjective simultaneity. *I-Perception, 8*(4), 204166951771929. https://doi.org/10.1177/2041669517719297

Arnal, L. H., Doelling, K. B., & Poeppel, D. (2015). Delta–Beta coupled oscillations underlie temporal prediction accuracy. *Cerebral Cortex, 25*(9), 3077–85. https://doi.org/10.1093/cercor/bhu103

Arnal, L. H., & Giraud, A.-L. (2012). Cortical oscillations and sensory predictions. *Trends in Cognitive Sciences, 16*(7), 390–8. https://doi.org/10.1016/J.TICS.2012.05.003

Azañón, E., & Soto-Faraco, S. (2008). Changing reference frames during the encoding of tactile events (DOI:10.1016/j.cub.2008.06.045). *Current Biology, 18*(16). https://doi.org/10.1016/j.cub.2008.08.008

Bach-y-Rita, P., Danilov, Y., Tyler, M. E., & Grimm, R. J. (2005). Late human brain plasticity: vestibular substitution with a tongue BrainPort human–machine interface. *Intellectica. Revue de l'Association Pour La Recherche Cognitive, 40*(1), 115–22. https://doi.org/10.3406/intel.2005.1362

Bach-y-Rita, P., & Kercel, S. W. (2003). Sensory substitution and the human–machine interface. *Trends in Cognitive Sciences, 7*(12), 541–6. https://doi.org/10.1016/J.TICS.2003.10.013

Beauchamp, M. S., Argall, B. D., Bodurka, J., Duyn, J. H., & Martin, A. (2004). Unraveling multisensory integration: patchy organization within human STS multisensory cortex. *Nature Neuroscience, 7*(11), 1190–2. https://doi.org/10.1038/nn1333

Beauchamp, M. S., Lee, K. E., Argall, B. D., & Martin, A. (2004). Integration of auditory and visual information about objects in superior temporal sulcus. *Neuron, 41*(5), 809–23. https://doi.org/10.1016/S0896–6273(04)00070–4

Beierholm, U. R., Quartz, S. R., & Shams, L. (2009). Bayesian priors are encoded independently from likelihoods in human multisensory perception. *Journal of Vision, 9*(5), 23. https://doi.org/10.1167/9.5.23

Benoit, M. M., Raij, T., Lin, F., Jääskeläinen, I. P., & Stufflebeam, S. (2010). Primary and multisensory cortical activity is correlated with audiovisual percepts. *Human Brain Mapping, 31*(4), 526–38.

Bernstein, L. E., Auer, E. T., Wagner, M., & Ponton, C. W. (2008). Spatiotemporal dynamics of audiovisual speech processing. *NeuroImage, 39*(1), 423–35. https://doi.org/10.1016/J.NEUROIMAGE.2007.08.035

Bernstein, L. E., Lu, Z.-L., & Jiang, J. (2008). Quantified acoustic–optical speech signal incongruity identifies cortical sites of audiovisual speech processing. *Brain Research, 1242*, 172–84.

Bertelson, P. (1998). Starting from the ventriloquist: The perception of multimodal events. In *Advances in psychological science, Vol. 2: Biological and cognitive aspects* (pp. 419–39). Hove, England: Psychology Press/Erlbaum (UK): Taylor & Francis.

Bertelson, P., & Aschersleben, G. (1998). Automatic visual bias of perceived auditory location. *Psychonomic Bulletin & Review, 5*(3), 482–9.

Bertelson, P., Vroomen, J., De Gelder, B., & Driver, J. (2000). The ventriloquist effect does not depend on the direction of deliberate visual attention. *Perception & Psychophysics*, *62*(2), 321–32. https://doi.org/10.3758/BF03205552

Biau, E. (2015). *Beat gestures and speech processing: when prosody extends to the speaker's hands*. Universitat Pompeu Fabra.

Biau, E., Fromont, L. A., & Soto-Faraco, S. (2018). Beat Gestures and Syntactic Parsing: an ERP Study. *Language Learning*, *68*, 102–26. https://doi.org/10.1111/lang.12257

Biau, E., Morís Fernández, L., Holle, H., Avila, C., & Soto-Faraco, S. (2016). Hand gestures as visual prosody: BOLD responses to audio-visual alignment are modulated by the communicative nature of the stimuli. *NeuroImage*, *132*. https://doi.org/10.1016/j.neuroimage.2016.02.018

Biau, E., & Soto-Faraco, S. (2013). Beat gestures modulate auditory integration in speech perception. *Brain and Language*, *124*(2). https://doi.org/10.1016/j.bandl.2012.10.008

Biau, E., & Soto-Faraco, S. (2015). Synchronization by the hand: the sight of gestures modulates low-frequency activity in brain responses to continuous speech. *Frontiers in Human Neuroscience*, *9*(September). https://doi.org/10.3389/fnhum.2015.00527

Biau, E., Torralba, M., Fuentemilla, L., de Diego Balaguer, R., & Soto-Faraco, S. (2015). Speaker's hand gestures modulate speech perception through phase resetting of ongoing neural oscillations. *Cortex*, *68*. https://doi.org/10.1016/j.cortex.2014.11.018

Birmingham, E., & Kingstone, A. (2009). Human social attention. *Annals of the New York Academy of Sciences*, *1156*(1), 118–40. https://doi.org/10.1111/j.1749-6632.2009.04468.x

Bizley, J. K., Maddox, R. K., & Lee, A. K. C. (2016). Defining auditory-visual objects: behavioral tests and physiological mechanisms. *Trends in Neurosciences*, *39*(2), 74–85. https://doi.org/10.1016/J.TINS.2015.12.007

Blanton, H., & Jaccard, J. (2006). Arbitrary metrics in psychology. *American Psychologist*, *61*(1), 27–41. https://doi.org/10.1037/0003-066X.61.1.27

Bolognini, N., Frassinetti, F., Serino, A., & Làdavas, E. (2005). 'Acoustical vision' of below threshold stimuli: interaction among spatially converging audiovisual inputs. *Experimental Brain Research*, *160*(3), 273–82. https://doi.org/10.1007/s00221-004-2005-z

Bordier, C., Puja, F., & Macaluso, E. (2013). Sensory processing during viewing of cinematographic material: computational modeling and functional neuroimaging. *NeuroImage*, *67*, 213–26. https://doi.org/10.1016/J.NEUROIMAGE.2012.11.031

Botvinick, M. M. (2007). Conflict monitoring and decision making: reconciling two perspectives on anterior cingulate function. *Cognitive, Affective, & Behavioral Neuroscience, 7*(4), 356–66.

Botvinick, M. M., Braver, T. S., Barch, D. M., Carter, C. S., & Cohen, J. D. (2001). Conflict monitoring and cognitive control. *Psychological Review, 108*(3), 624–52.

Botvinick, M. M., & Cohen, J. D. (1998). Rubber hands 'feel' touch that eyes see. *Nature, 391*(6669), 756.

Botvinick, M. M., Cohen, J. D., & Carter, C. S. (2004). Conflict monitoring and anterior cingulate cortex: an update. *Trends in Cognitive Sciences, 8*(12), 539–46. https://doi.org/10.1016/J.TICS.2004.10.003

Bronkhorst, A. W. (2000). The Cocktail Party phenomenon: a review of research on speech intelligibility in multiple-talker conditions. *Acta Acustica, 86*(1), 117–28.

Burgess, P. W., Alderman, N., Forbes, C., Costello, A., Coates, L. M-A., Dawson, D. R., . . . Channon, S. (2006). The case for the development and use of 'ecologically valid' measures of executive function in experimental and clinical neuropsychology. *Journal of the International Neuropsychological Society, 12*(02), 194–209. https://doi.org/10.1017/S1355617706060310

Busse, L., Roberts, K. C., Crist, R. E., Weissman, D. H., & Woldorff, M. G. (2005). The spread of attention across modalities and space in a multisensory object. *Proceedings of the National Academy of Sciences of the United States of America, 102*(51), 18751–18756.

Buzsáki, G. (2006). *Rhythms of the brain.* Oxford University Press.

Caclin, A., Bouchet, P., Djoulah, F., Pirat, E., Pernier, J., & Giard, M.-H. (2011). Auditory enhancement of visual perception at threshold depends on visual abilities. *Brain Research, 1396*, 35–44. https://doi.org/10.1016/J.BRAINRES.2011.04.016

Calvert, G., Spence, C., & Stein, B. E. (2004). *The handbook of multisensory processes.* Massachusetts Institute of Technology Press.

Castro, L., Soto-Faraco, S., Morís Fernández, L., & Ruzzoli, M. (2018). The breakdown of the Simon effect in cross-modal contexts: EEG evidence. *European Journal of Neuroscience, 47*(7). https://doi.org/10.1111/ejn.13882

Cavallina, C., Puccio, G., Capurso, M., Bremner, A. J., & Santangelo, V. (2018). Cognitive development attenuates audiovisual distraction and promotes the selection of task-relevant perceptual saliency during visual search on complex scenes. *Cognition, 180*, 91–8. https://doi.org/10.1016/J.COGNITION.2018.07.003

Cecere, R., Rees, G., & Romei, V. (2015). Individual differences in alpha frequency drive crossmodal illusory perception. *Current Biology, 25*(2), 231–5. https://doi.org/10.1016/J.CUB.2014.11.034

Chandrasekaran, C., Trubanova, A., Stillittano, S., Caplier, A., & Ghazanfar, A. A. (2009). The natural statistics of audiovisual speech. *PLoS Computational Biology*, *5*(7), e1000436. https://doi.org/10.1371/journal .pcbi.1000436

Chen, Y.-C., & Spence, C. (2010). When hearing the bark helps to identify the dog: semantically-congruent sounds modulate the identification of masked pictures. *Cognition*, *114*(3), 389–404. https://doi.org/10.1016/J.COGNITION.2009.10 .012

Chen, Y.-C., & Spence, C. (2011). Crossmodal semantic priming by naturalistic sounds and spoken words enhances visual sensitivity. *Journal of Experimental Psychology: Human Perception and Performance*, *37*(5), 1554–68. https://doi.org/10.1037/a0024329

Chen, Y.-C., & Spence, C. (2013). The time-course of the cross-modal semantic modulation of visual picture processing by naturalistic sounds and spoken words. *Multisensory Research*, *26*(4), 371–86. https://doi.org/10.1163 /22134808–00002420

Chen, Y.-C., & Spence, C. (2017). Assessing the role of the 'unity assumption' on multisensory integration: a review. *Frontiers in Psychology*, *8*, 445. https://doi.org/10.3389/fpsyg.2017.00445

Chen, Y.-C., & Spence, C. (2018a). Audiovisual semantic interactions between linguistic and nonlinguistic stimuli: the time-courses and categorical specificity. *Journal of Experimental Psychology: Human Perception and Performance*, *44*(10), 1488–507. https://doi.org/10.1037/xhp0000545

Chen, Y.-C., & Spence, C. (2018b). Dissociating the time courses of the cross-modal semantic priming effects elicited by naturalistic sounds and spoken words. *Psychonomic Bulletin & Review*, *25*(3), 1138–46. https://doi .org/10.3758/s13423-017–1324–6

Cherry, E. C. (1953). Some experiments on the recognition of speech, with one and with two ears. *The Journal of the Acoustical Society of America*, *25*(5), 975–9. https://doi.org/10.1121/1.1907229

Churchland, P. S., Ramachandran, V. S., & Sejnowski, T. J. (2005). A critique of pure vision. In C. Koch and J. Davis (Eds.), *Large-Scale Neuronal Theories of the Brain*, 1–25. https://doi.org/10.1207/S15326969ECO1502_5

Clayton, M. S., Yeung, N., & Cohen Kadosh, R. (2015). The roles of cortical oscillations in sustained attention. *Trends in Cognitive Sciences*, *19*(4), 188–95. https://doi.org/10.1016/J.TICS.2015.02.004

Colonius, H., & Arndt, P. (2001). A two-stage model for visual-auditory inter-action in saccadic latencies. *Perception & Psychophysics*, *63*(1), 126–47. https://doi.org/10.3758/BF03200508

Colonius, H., & Diederich, A. (2004). Multisensory interaction in saccadic reaction time: a time-window-of-integration model. *Journal of Cognitive Neuroscience, 16*(6), 1000–9. https://doi.org/10.1162/0898929041502733

Connor, S. (2000). *Dumbstruck: a cultural history of ventriloquism.* Oxford University Press. https://doi.org/10.1093/acprof:oso/9780198184331.001.0001

Corneil, B. D., Van Wanrooij, M., Munoz, D. P., & Van Opstal, A. J. (2002). Auditory-visual interactions subserving goal-directed saccades in a complex scene. *Journal of Neurophysiology, 88*(1), 438–54. https://doi.org/10.1152/jn.2002.88.1.438

Dalton, P., Doolittle, N., Nagata, H., & Breslin, P. A. S. (2000). The merging of the senses: integration of subthreshold taste and smell. *Nature Neuroscience, 3*(5), 431–2. https://doi.org/10.1038/74797

Danilov, Y., & Tyler, M. E. (2005). Brainport: an alternative input to the brain. *Journal of Integrative Neuroscience, 04*(04), 537–50. https://doi.org/10.1142/S0219635205000914

De Gelder, B., & Bertelson, P. (2003). Multisensory integration, perception and ecological validity. *Trends in Cognitive Sciences, 7*(10), 460–7. https://doi.org/10.1016/J.TICS.2003.08.014

De Meo, R., Murray, M. M., Clarke, S., & Matusz, P. J. (2015). Top-down control and early multisensory processes: chicken vs. egg. *Frontiers in Integrative Neuroscience, 9*, 17. https://doi.org/10.3389/fnint.2015.00017

Desantis, A., & Haggard, P. (2016). Action-outcome learning and prediction shape the window of simultaneity of audiovisual outcomes. *Cognition, 153*, 33–42. https://doi.org/10.1016/j.cognition.2016.03.009

Desimone, R., & Duncan, J. (1995). Neural mechanisms of selective visual attention. *Annual Review of Neuroscience, 18*(1), 193–222.

Diederich, A., & Colonius, H. (2004). Bimodal and trimodal multisensory enhancement: Effects of stimulus onset and intensity on reaction time. *Perception & Psychophysics, 66*(8), 1388–404. https://doi.org/10.3758/BF03195006

Dimitrova, D., Chu, M., Wang, L., Özyürek, A., & Hagoort, P. (2016). Beat that word: how listeners integrate beat gesture and focus in multimodal speech discourse. *Journal of Cognitive Neuroscience, 28*(9), 1255–69. https://doi.org/10.1162/jocn_a_00963

Doehrmann, O., & Naumer, M. J. (2008). Semantics and the multisensory brain: How meaning modulates processes of audio-visual integration. *Brain Research, 1242*, 136–50. https://doi.org/10.1016/J.BRAINRES.2008.03.071

Donohue, S. E., Green, J. J., & Woldorff, M. G. (2015). The effects of attention on the temporal integration of multisensory stimuli. *Frontiers in Integrative Neuroscience, 9*, 32. https://doi.org/10.3389/fnint.2015.00032

Driver, J. (1996). Enhancement of selective listening by illusory mislocation of speech sounds due to lip-reading. *Nature, 381*(6577), 66–8. https://doi.org/10 .1038/381066a0

Driver, J., & Noesselt, T. (2008). Multisensory interplay reveals crossmodal influences on 'sensory-specific' brain regions, neural responses, and judgments. *Neuron, 57*(1), 11–23. https://doi.org/10.1016/J.NEURON.2007.12.013

Driver, J., & Spence, C. (1994). Spatial synergies between auditory and visual attention. In Umilta, C and Moscovitch, M (eds.), *Attention and Performance 15* (pp. 311–31). Cambridge, MA: Massachusetts Institute of Technology Press.

Driver, J., & Spence, C. (1998). Attention and the crossmodal construction of space. *Trends in Cognitive Sciences, 2*(7), 254–62. https://doi.org/10.1016 /S1364–6613(98)01188–7

Driver, J., & Spence, C. (2000). Multisensory perception: beyond modularity and convergence. *Current Biology, 10*(20), R731–R735. https://doi.org/10 .1016/S0960–9822(00)00740–5

Duncan, J., Martens, S., & Ward, R. (1997). Restricted attentional capacity within but not between sensory modalities. *Nature, 387*(6635), 808–10. https://doi.org/10.1038/42947

Durie, B. (2005). Doors of perception. *New Scientist, 185*(2484), 34–6.

Enns, J. T., & Lleras, A. (2008). What's next? New evidence for prediction in human vision. *Trends in Cognitive Sciences, 12*(9), 327–33. https://doi.org /10.1016/J.TICS.2008.06.001

Eriksen, B. A., & Eriksen, C. W. (1974). Effects of noise letters upon the identification of a target letter in a nonsearch task. *Perception & Psychophysics, 16*(1), 143–9. https://doi.org/10.3758/BF03203267

Ernst, M. O., & Banks, M. S. (2002). Humans integrate visual and haptic information in a statistically optimal fashion. *Nature, 415*(6870), 429–33. https://doi.org/10.1038/415429a

Fairhall, S. L., & Macaluso, E. (2009). Spatial attention can modulate audio-visual integration at multiple cortical and subcortical sites. *European Journal of Neuroscience, 29*(6), 1247–57. https://doi.org/10.1111/j.1460–9568 .2009.06688.x

Falchier, A., Clavagnier, S., Barone, P., & Kennedy, H. (2002). Anatomical evidence of multimodal integration in primate striate cortex. *The Journal of Neuroscience, 22*(13), 5749 LP–5759.

Fetsch, C. R., Pouget, A., DeAngelis, G. C., & Angelaki, D. E. (2012). Neural correlates of reliability-based cue weighting during multisensory integration. *Nature Neuroscience, 15*(1), 146–54. https://doi.org/10.1038/nn.2983

Fiebelkorn, I. C., Foxe, J. J., Butler, J. S., Mercier, M. R., Snyder, A. C., & Molholm, S. (2011). Ready, set, reset: stimulus-locked periodicity in behavioral performance demonstrates the consequences of cross-sensory phase reset. *The Journal of Neuroscience, 31*(27),9971 LP–9981.

Fiebelkorn, I. C., Foxe, J. J., Schwartz, T. H., & Molholm, S. (2010). Staying within the lines: the formation of visuospatial boundaries influences multisensory feature integration. *European Journal of Neuroscience, 31*(10), 1737–43. https://doi.org/10.1111/j.1460–9568.2010.07196.x

Folk, C. L., Remington, R. W., & Johnston, J. C. (1992). Involuntary covert orienting is contingent on attentional control settings. *Journal of Experimental Psychology. Human Perception and Performance, 18*(4), 1030–44. https://doi .org/10.1037//0096–1523.18.4.1015

Foxe, J. J., Morocz, I. A., Murray, M. M., Higgins, B. A., Javitt, D. C., & Schroeder, C. E. (2000). Multisensory auditory–somatosensory interactions in early cortical processing revealed by high-density electrical mapping. *Cognitive Brain Research, 10*(1–2), 77–83. https://doi.org/10.1016/S0926–6410(00) 00024–0

Foxe, J. J., & Schroeder, C. E. (2005). The case for feedforward multisensory convergence during early cortical processing. *Neuroreport, 16*(5), 419–23.

Frassinetti, F., Bolognini, N., & Làdavas, E. (2002). Enhancement of visual perception by crossmodal visuo-auditory interaction. *Experimental Brain Research, 147*(3), 332–43. https://doi.org/10.1007/s00221-002–1262–y

Friston, K. (2005). A theory of cortical responses. *Philosophical Transactions of the Royal Society B: Biological Sciences, 360*(1456), 815–836.

Friston, K. (2010). The free-energy principle: a unified brain theory? *Nature Reviews Neuroscience, 11*(2), 127–38. https://doi.org/10.1038 /nrn2787

Fujisaki, W., Koene, A., Arnold, D. H., Johnston, A., & Nishida, S. (2006). Visual search for a target changing in synchrony with an auditory signal. *Proceedings. Biological Sciences, 273*(1588), 865–74. https://doi.org/10 .1098/rspb.2005.3327

Fujisaki, W., & Nishida, S. (2010). A common perceptual temporal limit of binding synchronous inputs across different sensory attributes and modalities. *Proceedings of the Royal Society B: Biological Sciences.* http://doi.org /10.1098/rspb.2010.0243

Fujisaki, W., Shimojo, S., Kashino, M., & Nishida, S. (2004). Recalibration of audiovisual simultaneity. *Nature Neuroscience, 7*(7), 773–8. https://doi.org/10 .1038/nn1268

Gallivan, J. P., Chapman, C. S., Wolpert, D. M., & Flanagan, J. R. (2018). Decision-making in sensorimotor control. *Nature Reviews Neuroscience, 19*(9), 519–34. https://doi.org/10.1038/s41583-018–0045–9

Gau, R., & Noppeney, U. (2016). How prior expectations shape multisensory perception. *NeuroImage*, *124*, 876–86. https://doi.org/10.1016/J.NEUROIMAG E.2015.09.045

Ghazanfar, A. A., & Schroeder, C. E. (2006). Is neocortex essentially multisensory? *Trends in Cognitive Sciences*, 10(6), 278–85. https://doi.org /10.1016/J.TICS.2006.04.008

Gleiss, S., & Kayser, C. (2013). Eccentricity dependent auditory enhancement of visual stimulus detection but not discrimination. *Frontiers in Integrative Neuroscience*, *7*, 52. https://doi.org/10.3389/fnint.2013.00052

Gleiss, S., & Kayser, C. (2014). Acoustic noise improves visual perception and modulates occipital oscillatory states. *Journal of Cognitive Neuroscience*, *26*(4), 699–711. https://doi.org/10.1162/jocn_a_00524

Grabot, L., Kösem, A., Azizi, L., & van Wassenhove, V. (2017). Prestimulus alpha oscillations and the temporal sequencing of audiovisual events. *Journal of Cognitive Neuroscience*, *29*(9), 1566–82. https://doi.org/10.1162/jocn_a_01145

Grant, K. W., & Seitz, P.-F. (2000). The use of visible speech cues for improving auditory detection of spoken sentences. *The Journal of the Acoustical Society of America*, *108*(3), 1197. https://doi.org/10.1121/1.1288668

Hartcher-O'Brien, J., Soto-Faraco, S., & Adam, R. (2017). Editorial: a matter of bottom-up or top-down processes: the role of attention in multisensory integration. *Frontiers in Integrative Neuroscience*, *11*. https://doi.org/10 .3389/fnint.2017.00005

Hartcher-O'Brien, J., Talsma, D., Adam, R., Vercillo, T., Macaluso, E., & Noppeney, U. (2016). The curious incident of attention in multisensory integration: bottom-up vs. top-down. *Multisensory Research*, *29*(6–7), 557–83. https://doi.org/10.1163/22134808–00002528

Hasbroucq, T., & Guiard, Y. (1991). Stimulus-response compatibility and the Simon effect: toward a conceptual clarification. *Journal of Experimental Psychology: Human Perception and Performance*, *17*(1), 246–66.

Hasson, U., Malach, R., & Heeger, D. J. (2010). Reliability of cortical activity during natural stimulation. *Trends in Cognitive Sciences*, *14*(1), 40–8. https:// doi.org/10.1016/J.TICS.2009.10.011

Hasson, U., Nir, Y., Levy, I., Fuhrmann, G., & Malach, R. (2004). Intersubject synchronization of cortical activity during natural vision. *Science*, *303*(5664), 1634 LP–1640.

Hasson, U., Skipper, J. I., Nusbaum, H. C., & Small, S. L. (2007). Abstract coding of audiovisual speech: beyond sensory representation. *Neuron*, *56*(6), 1116–26.

Heed, T., Buchholz, V. N., Engel, A. K., & Röder, B. (2015). Tactile remapping: from coordinate transformation to integration in sensorimotor processing. *Trends in Cognitive Sciences*, *19*(5), 251–8. https://doi.org/10.1016/J.TICS.2015.03.001

Heron, J., Roach, N. W., Hanson, J. V. M., McGraw, P. V, & Whitaker, D. (2012). Audiovisual time perception is spatially specific. *Experimental Brain Research*, *218*(3), 477–85. https://doi.org/10.1007/s00221-012-3038-3

Hipp, J. F., Engel, A. K., & Siegel, M. (2011). Oscillatory synchronization in large-scale cortical networks predicts perception. *Neuron*, *69*(2), 387–96. https://doi.org/10.1016/J.NEURON.2010.12.027

Ho, C., Reed, N., & Spence, C. (2006). Assessing the effectiveness of 'intuitive' vibrotactile warning signals in preventing front-to-rear-end collisions in a driving simulator. *Accident Analysis & Prevention*, *38*(5), 988–96. https://doi.org/10.1016/J.AAP.2006.04.002

Ho, C., Reed, N., & Spence, C. (2007). Multisensory in-car warning signals for collision avoidance. *Human Factors: The Journal of the Human Factors and Ergonomics Society*, *49*(6), 1107–14. https://doi.org/10.1518/001872007X249965

Ho, C., & Spence, C. (2014). Effectively responding to tactile stimulation: Do homologous cue and effector locations really matter? *Acta Psychologica*, *151*, 32–9. https://doi.org/10.1016/J.ACTPSY.2014.05.014

Ho, C., Tan, H. Z., & Spence, C. (2005). Using spatial vibrotactile cues to direct visual attention in driving scenes. *Transportation Research Part F: Traffic Psychology and Behaviour*, *8*(6), 397–412. https://doi.org/10.1016/J.TRF.2005.05.002

Holle, H., Obermeier, C., Schmidt-Kassow, M., Friederici, A. D., Ward, J., & Gunter, T. C. (2012). Gesture facilitates the syntactic analysis of speech. *Frontiers in Psychology*, *3*, 74. https://doi.org/10.3389/fpsyg.2012.00074

Hommel, B. (1993). The role of attention for the Simon effect. *Psychological Research*, *55*(3), 208–22.

Hommel, B. (2011). The Simon effect as tool and heuristic. *Acta Psychologica*, *136*(2), 189–202.

Huang, L., Treisman, A., & Pashler, H. (2007). Characterizing the limits of human visual awareness. *Science*, *317*(5839), 823–825.

Hubbard, A. L., Wilson, S. M., Callan, D. E., & Dapretto, M. (2009). Giving speech a hand: gesture modulates activity in auditory cortex during speech perception. *Human Brain Mapping*, *30*(3), 1028–37. https://doi.org/10.1002/hbm.20565

Igualada, A., Esteve-Gibert, N., & Prieto, P. (2017). Beat gestures improve word recall in 3- to 5-year-old children. *Journal of Experimental Child Psychology*, *156*, 99–112. https://doi.org/10.1016/J.JECP.2016.11.017

Ikumi, N., & Soto-Faraco, S. (2014). Selective attention modulates the direction of audio-visual temporal recalibration. *PLoS ONE*, *9*(7). https://doi.org/10.1371/journal.pone.0099311

Ikumi, N., & Soto-Faraco, S. (2017). Grouping and segregation of sensory events by actions in temporal audio-visual recalibration. *Frontiers in Integrative Neuroscience, 10*. https://doi.org/10.3389/fnint.2016.00044

Ikumi, N., Torralba, M., Ruzzoli, M., & Soto-Faraco, S. (2019). The phase of pre-stimulus brain oscillations correlates with cross-modal synchrony perception. *European Journal of Neuroscience, 49*(2), 150–64. https://doi.org/10.1111/ejn.14186

Iordanescu, L., Grabowecky, M., Franconeri, S., Theeuwes, J., & Suzuki, S. (2010). Characteristic sounds make you look at target objects more quickly. *Attention, Perception & Psychophysics, 72*(7), 1736–41. https://doi.org/10.3758/APP.72.7.1736

Iordanescu, L., Grabowecky, M., & Suzuki, S. (2011). Object-based auditory facilitation of visual search for pictures and words with frequent and rare targets. *Acta Psychologica, 137*(2), 252–9. https://doi.org/10.1016/J.ACTPSY.2010.07.017

Iordanescu, L., Guzman-Martinez, E., Grabowecky, M., & Suzuki, S. (2008). Characteristic sounds facilitate visual search. *Psychonomic Bulletin & Review, 15*(3), 548–54. https://doi.org/10.3758/PBR.15.3.548

Jack, B. N., O'Shea, R. P., Cottrell, D., & Ritter, W. (2013). Does the ventriloquist illusion assist selective listening? *Journal of Experimental Psychology: Human Perception and Performance, 39*(5), 1496–502. https://doi.org/10.1037/a0033594

Jaekl, P. M., & Harris, L. R. (2009). Sounds can affect visual perception mediated primarily by the parvocellular pathway. *Visual Neuroscience, 26*(5–6), 477–86. https://doi.org/10.1017/S0952523809990289

Jaekl, P. M., Pérez-Bellido, A., & Soto-Faraco, S. (2014). On the 'visual' in 'audio-visual integration': a hypothesis concerning visual pathways. *Experimental Brain Research, 232*(6), 1631–8. https://doi.org/10.1007/s00221-014-3927-8

Jaekl, P. M., Pesquita, A., Sinnett, S., Alsius, A., Munhall, K., & Soto-Faraco, S. (2015). The contribution of dynamic visual cues to audiovisual speech perception. *Neuropsychologia, 75*, 402–10.

Jaekl, P. M., & Soto-Faraco, S. (2010). Audiovisual contrast enhancement is articulated primarily via the M-pathway. *Brain Research, 1366*, 85–92. https://doi.org/10.1016/j.brainres.2010.10.012

Jiang, J., Zhang, Q., & Van Gaal, S. (2015). EEG neural oscillatory dynamics reveal semantic and response conflict at difference levels of conflict awareness. *Scientific Reports, 5*, 12008.

Kayser, C., Körding, K. P., & König, P. (2004). Processing of complex stimuli and natural scenes in the visual cortex. *Current Opinion in Neurobiology, 14*(4), 468–73. https://doi.org/10.1016/J.CONB.2004.06.002

Kayser, C., & Shams, L. (2015). Multisensory causal inference in the brain. *PLOS Biology*, *13*(2), e1002075. https://doi.org/10.1371/journal.pbio.1002075

Keil, J., Müller, N., Hartmann, T., & Weisz, N. (2014). Prestimulus beta power and phase synchrony influence the sound-induced flash illusion. *Cerebral Cortex*, *24*(5), 1278–88.

Keil, J., & Senkowski, D. (2017). Individual alpha frequency relates to the sound-induced flash illusion. *Multisensory Research*, *30*(6), 565–78. https://doi.org/10.1163/22134808–00002572

King, A. J. (2005). Multisensory integration: strategies for synchronization. *Current Biology*, *15*(9), R339–R341. https://doi.org/10.1016/J.CUB.2005.04.022

Kingstone, A., Smilek, D., Ristic, J., Kelland Friesen, C., & Eastwood, J. D. (2003). Attention, researchers! It is time to take a look at the real world. *Current Directions in Psychological Science*, *12*(5), 176–80. https://doi.org/10.1111/1467–8721.01255

Kitano, H. (2002). Systems biology: a brief overview. *Science (New York, N.Y.)*, *295*(5560), 1662–4. https://doi.org/10.1126/science.1069492

Knoeferle, K. M., Knoeferle, P., Velasco, C., & Spence, C. (2016). Multisensory brand search: how the meaning of sounds guides consumers' visual attention. *Journal of Experimental Psychology: Applied*, *22*(2), 196–210. https://doi.org/10.1037/xap0000084

Koelewijn, T., Bronkhorst, A., & Theeuwes, J. (2010). Attention and the multiple stages of multisensory integration: a review of audiovisual studies. *Acta Psychologica*, *134*(3), 372–84. https://doi.org/10.1016/J.ACTPSY.2010.03.010

Kösem, A., Gramfort, A., & van Wassenhove, V. (2014). Encoding of event timing in the phase of neural oscillations. *NeuroImage*, *92*, 274–84. https://doi.org/10.1016/J.NEUROIMAGE.2014.02.010

Kösem, A., & van Wassenhove, V. (2012). Temporal structure in audiovisual sensory selection. *PLoS ONE*, *7*(7), e40936. https://doi.org/10.1371/journal.pone.0040936

Kvasova, D., Garcia-Vernet, L., & Soto-Faraco, S. (2019). Characteristic sounds facilitate object search in real-life scenes. *bioRxiv*, 563080. doi: https://doi.org/10.1101/563080

Ladavas, E., & Moscovitch, M. (1984). Must egocentric and environmental frames of reference be aligned to produce spatial S-R compatibility effects? *Journal of Experimental Psychology: Human Perception and Performance*. American Psychological Association. https://doi.org/10.1037/0096–1523.10.2.205

Lakatos, P., Chen, C.-M., O'Connell, M. N., Mills, A., & Schroeder, C. E. (2007). Neuronal oscillations and multisensory interaction in primary auditory cortex. *Neuron*, *53*(2), 279–92. https://doi.org/10.1016/J.NEURON.2006.12.011

Lakatos, P., Karmos, G., Mehta, A. D., Ulbert, I., & Schroeder, C. E. (2008). Entrainment of neuronal oscillations as a mechanism of attentional selection. *Science, 320*(5872), 110–113.

Lamberts, K., Tavernier, G., & d'Ydewalle, G. (1992). Effects of multiple reference points in spatial stimulus-response compatibility. *Acta Psychologica, 79*(2), 115–30.

Laurienti, P., Kraft, R., Maldjian, J., Burdette, J., & Wallace, M. (2004). Semantic congruence is a critical factor in multisensory behavioral performance. *Experimental Brain Research, 158*(4), 405–14. https://doi.org/10.1007/s00221-004-1913-2

Leone, L. M., & McCourt, M. E. (2013). The roles of physical and physiological simultaneity in audiovisual multisensory facilitation. *I-Perception, 4*(4), 213–28. https://doi.org/10.1068/i0532

Lewald, J., & Guski, R. (2003). Cross-modal perceptual integration of spatially and temporally disparate auditory and visual stimuli. *Cognitive Brain Research, 16*(3), 468–78. https://doi.org/10.1016/S0926-6410(03)00074-0

Lippert, M., Logothetis, N. K., & Kayser, C. (2007). Improvement of visual contrast detection by a simultaneous sound. *Brain Research, 1173*, 102–9. https://doi.org/10.1016/J.BRAINRES.2007.07.050

Lunghi, C., & Alais, D. (2013). Touch interacts with vision during binocular rivalry with a tight orientation tuning. *PLoS ONE, 8*(3), e58754. https://doi.org/10.1371/journal.pone.0058754

Lunn, J., Sjoblom, A., Ward, J., Soto-Faraco, S., & Forster, S. (2019). Multisensory enhancement of attention depends on whether you are already paying attention. *Cognition, 187*, 38–49. https://doi.org/10.1016/J.COGNITION.2019.02.008

Macaluso, E., & Doricchi, F. (2013). Attention and predictions: control of spatial attention beyond the endogenous-exogenous dichotomy. *Frontiers in Human Neuroscience, 7*, 685. https://doi.org/10.3389/fnhum.2013.00685

Macaluso, E., & Driver, J. (2005). Multisensory spatial interactions: a window onto functional integration in the human brain. *Trends in Neurosciences, 28*(5), 264–71. https://doi.org/10.1016/J.TINS.2005.03.008

Macaluso, E., Frith, C. D., & Driver, J. (2000). Modulation of human visual cortex by crossmodal spatial attention. *Science (New York, N.Y.), 289*(5482), 1206–8. https://doi.org/10.1126/science.289.5482.1206

MacLeod, C. M. (1991). Half a century of research on the Stroop effect: An integrative review. *Psychological Bulletin, 109*(2), 163–203. https://doi.org/10.1037/0033-2909.109.2.163

Maddox, R. K., Atilgan, H., Bizley, J. K., & Lee, A. K. (2015). Auditory selective attention is enhanced by a task-irrelevant temporally coherent visual stimulus in human listeners. *ELife, 4*, 4995.

Maguire, E. A. (2012). Studying the freely-behaving brain with fMRI. *NeuroImage, 62*(2), 1170–6. https://doi.org/10.1016/J .NEUROIMAGE.2012.01.009

Maidenbaum, S., & Abboud, S. (2014). Sensory substitution: closing the gap between basic research and widespread practical visual rehabilitation. *Neuroscience & Biobehavioral Reviews, 41*, 3–15. https://doi.org/10.1016/J .NEUBIOREV.2013.11.007

Malfait, N., Fonlupt, P., Centelles, L., Nazarian, B., Brown, L. E., & Caclin, A. (2014). Different neural networks are involved in audiovisual speech perception depending on the context. *Journal of Cognitive Neuroscience, 26*(7), 1572–86.

Martolini, C., Cuppone, A. V., Cappagli, G., Finocchietti, S., Maviglia, A., & Gori, M. (2018). ABBI-K: a novel tool for evaluating spatial and motor abilities in visually impaired children. In *2018 IEEE International Symposium on Medical Measurements and Applications (MeMeA)* (pp. 1–6). IEEE. https://doi.org/10.1109/MeMeA.2018.8438671

Mast, F., Frings, C., & Spence, C. (2017). Crossmodal attentional control sets between vision and audition. *Acta Psychologica, 178*, 41–7. https://doi.org /10.1016/J.ACTPSY.2017.05.011

Mastroberardino, S., Santangelo, V., & Macaluso, E. (2015). Crossmodal semantic congruence can affect visuo-spatial processing and activity of the fronto-parietal attention networks. *Frontiers in Integrative Neuroscience, 9*, 45. https://doi.org/10.3389/fnint.2015.00045

Matchin, W., Groulx, K., & Hickok, G. (2014). Audiovisual speech integration does not rely on the motor system: evidence from articulatory suppression, the McGurk effect, and fMRI. *Journal of Cognitive Neuroscience, 26*(3), 606–20.

Matusz, P. J., Broadbent, H., Ferrari, J., Forrest, B., Merkley, R., & Scerif, G. (2015). Multi-modal distraction: insights from children's limited attention. *Cognition, 136*, 156–65. https://doi.org/10.1016/J .COGNITION.2014.11.031

Matusz, P. J., Dikker, S., Huth, A. G., & Perrodin, C. (2018). Are we ready for real-world neuroscience? *Journal of Cognitive Neuroscience*, 1–12. https:// doi.org/10.1162/jocn_e_01276

Matusz, P. J., & Eimer, M. (2011). Multisensory enhancement of attentional capture in visual search. *Psychonomic Bulletin & Review, 18*(5), 904–9. https://doi.org/10.3758/s13423-011-0131-8

Matusz, P. J., Turoman, N., Tivadar, R. I., Retsa, C., & Murray, M. M. (2019). Brain and cognitive mechanisms of top–down attentional control in a multisensory world: benefits of electrical neuroimaging. *Journal of Cognitive Neuroscience, 31*(3), 412–30. https://doi.org/10.1162/jocn_a_01360

McDonald, J. J., Teder-Sälejärvi, W. A., & Ward, L. M. (2001). Multisensory integration and crossmodal attention effects in the human brain. *Science*, *292*(5523), 1791.

McGurk, H., & MacDonald, J. (1976). Hearing lips and seeing voices. *Nature*, *264*(5588), 746.

McNeill, D. (1992). *Hand and mind: what gestures reveal about thought*. University of Chicago Press.

Medina, J., McCloskey, M., Coslett, H., & Rapp, B. (2014). Somatotopic representation of location: evidence from the Simon effect. *Journal of Experimental Psychology: Human Perception and Performance*, *40*(6), 2131–42.

Miller, J. (1982). Divided attention: evidence for coactivation with redundant signals. *Cognitive Psychology*, *14*(2), 247–79. https://doi.org/10.1016/0010-0285(82)90010-X

Miller, J. (1986). Timecourse of coactivation in bimodal divided attention. *Perception & Psychophysics*, *40*(5), 331–43. https://doi.org/10.3758/BF03203025

Miller, L. M., & D'esposito, M. (2005). Perceptual fusion and stimulus coincidence in the cross-modal integration of speech. *Journal of Neuroscience*, *25*(25), 5884–93.

Milton, A., & Pleydell-Pearce, C. W. (2016). The phase of pre-stimulus alpha oscillations influences the visual perception of stimulus timing. *NeuroImage*, *133*, 53–61. https://doi.org/10.1016/j.neuroimage.2016.02.065

Molholm, S., Ritter, W., Javitt, D. C., & Foxe, J. J. (2004). Multisensory visual–auditory object recognition in humans: a high-density electrical mapping study. *Cerebral Cortex*, *14*(4), 452–65.

Molholm, S., Ritter, W., Murray, M. M., Javitt, D. C., Schroeder, C. E., & Foxe, J. J. (2002). Multisensory auditory–visual interactions during early sensory processing in humans: a high-density electrical mapping study. *Cognitive Brain Research*, *14*(1), 115–28. https://doi.org/10.1016/S0926-6410(02)00066-6

Morein-Zamir, S., Soto-Faraco, S., & Kingstone, A. (2003). Auditory capture of vision: examining temporal ventriloquism. *Brain Research*, *17*(1), 154–63.

Morís Fernández, L., Macaluso, E., & Soto-Faraco, S. (2017). Audiovisual integration as conflict resolution: the conflict of the McGurk illusion. *Human Brain Mapping*, *38*(11). https://doi.org/10.1002/hbm.23758

Morís Fernández, L., Torralba, M., & Soto-Faraco, S. (2018). Theta oscillations reflect conflict processing in the perception of the McGurk illusion. *European Journal of Neuroscience*. https://doi.org/10.1111/ejn.13804

Morís Fernández, L., Visser, M., Ventura-Campos, N., Ávila, C., & Soto-Faraco, S. (2015). Top-down attention regulates the neural expression of audiovisual integration. *NeuroImage, 119*. https://doi.org/10.1016/j .neuroimage.2015.06.052

Murray, M. M., Molholm, S., Michel, C. M., Heslenfeld, D. J., Ritter, W., Javitt, D. C., ... Foxe, J. J. (2005). Grabbing your ear: rapid auditory–somatosensory multisensory interactions in low-level sensory cortices are not constrained by stimulus alignment. *Cerebral Cortex, 15*(7), 963–74. https://doi.org/10.1093/cercor/bhh197

Nahorna, O., Berthommier, F., & Schwartz, J.-L. (2012). Binding and unbinding the auditory and visual streams in the McGurk effect. *The Journal of the Acoustical Society of America, 132*(2), 1061–77. https://doi.org/10.1121/1.4728187

Nardo, D., Console, P., Reverberi, C., & Macaluso, E. (2016). Competition between visual events modulates the influence of salience during free-viewing of naturalistic videos. *Frontiers in Human Neuroscience, 10*, 320. https://doi.org/10.3389/fnhum.2016.00320

Nardo, D., Santangelo, V., & Macaluso, E. (2011). Stimulus-driven orienting of visuo-spatial attention in complex dynamic environments. *Neuron, 69*(5), 1015–28. https://doi.org/10.1016/J.NEURON.2011.02.020

Nardo, D., Santangelo, V., & Macaluso, E. (2014). Spatial orienting in complex audiovisual environments. *Human Brain Mapping, 35*(4), 1597–614. https:// doi.org/10.1002/hbm.22276

Navarra, J., Alsius, A., Soto-Faraco, S., & Spence, C. (2010). Assessing the role of attention in the audiovisual integration of speech. *Information Fusion, 11*(1), 4–11. https://doi.org/10.1016/j.inffus.2009.04.001

Navarra, J., Vatakis, A., Zampini, M., Soto-Faraco, S., Humphreys, W., & Spence, C. (2005). Exposure to asynchronous audiovisual speech extends the temporal window for audiovisual integration. *Brain Research, 25*(2), 499–507. https://doi.org/10.1016/J.COGBRAINRES.2005.07.009

Neisser, U. (1976). *Cognition and reality. Principles and implication of cognitive psychology.* San Francisco: WH Freeman and Company.

Neisser, U. (1982). Memory: what are the important questions? In J. U. Neisser & I. E. Hyman (eds.), *Memory observed* (pp. 3–18). New York: Worth.

Nelken, I., Bizley, J., Shamma, S. A., & Wang, X. (2014). Auditory cortical processing in real-world listening: the auditory system going real. *The Journal of Neuroscience: The Official Journal of the Society for Neuroscience, 34*(46), 15135–8. https://doi.org/10.1523/JNEUROSCI.2989–14.2014

Noesselt, T., Tyll, S., Boehler, C. N., Budinger, E., Heinze, H.-J., & Driver, J. (2010). Sound-induced enhancement of low-intensity vision: multisensory influences on human sensory-specific cortices and thalamic bodies relate to perceptual enhancement of visual detection sensitivity. *The Journal of Neuroscience*, *30*(41), 13609 LP–13623.

Noppeney, U., Josephs, O., Hocking, J., Price, C. J., & Friston, K. J. (2008). The effect of prior visual information on recognition of speech and sounds. *Cerebral Cortex*, *18*(3), 598–609. https://doi.org/10.1093/cercor/bhm091

Noppeney, U., & Lee, H. L. (2018). Causal inference and temporal predictions in audiovisual perception of speech and music. *Annals of the New York Academy of Sciences*, *1423*(1), 102–16. https://doi.org/10.1111/nyas.13615

O'Regan, J. K. (1992). Solving the 'real' mysteries of visual perception: The world as an outside memory. *Canadian Journal of Psychology/Revue Canadienne de Psychologie*, *46*(3), 461–88. https://doi.org/10.1037/h0084327

Odgaard, E. C., Arieh, Y., & Marks, L. E. (2003). Cross-modal enhancement of perceived brightness: sensory interaction versus response bias. *Perception & Psychophysics*, *65*(1), 123–32. https://doi.org/10.3758/BF03194789

Ojanen, V., Möttönen, R., Pekkola, J., Jääskeläinen, I. P., Joensuu, R., Autti, T., & Sams, M. (2005). Processing of audiovisual speech in Broca's area. *Neuroimage*, *25*(2), 333–8.

Otto, T. U., & Mamassian, P. (2012). Noise and correlations in parallel perceptual decision making. *Current Biology*, *22*(15), 1391–6. https://doi.org/10.1016/J.CUB.2012.05.031

Pannunzi, M., Pérez-Bellido, A., Pereda-Baños, A., López-Moliner, J., Deco, G., & Soto-Faraco, S. (2015). Deconstructing multisensory enhancement in detection. *Journal of Neurophysiology*, *113*(6). https://doi.org/10.1152/jn.00341.2014

Pápai, M. S., & Soto-Faraco, S. (2017). Sounds can boost the awareness of visual events through attention without cross-modal integration. *Scientific Reports*, *7*. https://doi.org/10.1038/srep41684

Papeo, L., Goupil, N. & Soto-Faraco, S. (2019, June 18). Visual search for people among people. *PsychRxiv*, https://doi.org/10.31234/osf.io/fupes

Parise, C. V., Knorre, K., & Ernst, M. O. (2014). Natural auditory scene statistics shapes human spatial hearing. *Proceedings of the National Academy of Sciences of the United States of America*, *111*(16), 6104–8. https://doi.org/10.1073/pnas.1322705111

Parise, C. V., & Spence, C. (2009). 'When birds of a feather flock together': synesthetic correspondences modulate audiovisual integration in non-synesthetes. *PLoS ONE*, *4*(5), e5664. https://doi.org/10.1371/journal.pone.0005664

Parise, C. V., Spence, C., & Ernst, M. O. (2012). When correlation implies causation in multisensory integration. *Current Biology*, *22*(1), 46–9. https://doi.org/10.1016/J.CUB.2011.11.039

Peelen, M. V., & Kastner, S. (2014). Attention in the real world: toward understanding its neural basis. *Trends in Cognitive Sciences*, *18*(5), 242–50. https://doi.org/10.1016/J.TICS.2014.02.004

Pekkola, J., Laasonen, M., Ojanen, V., Autti, T., Jääskeläinen, I. P., Kujala, T., & Sams, M. (2006). Perception of matching and conflicting audiovisual speech in dyslexic and fluent readers: an fMRI study at 3 T. *NeuroImage*, *29*(3), 797–807. https://doi.org/10.1016/J.NEUROIMAGE.2005.09.069

Pérez-Bellido, A., Soto-Faraco, S., & López-Moliner, J. (2013). Sound-driven enhancement of vision: disentangling detection-level from decision-level contributions. *Journal of Neurophysiology*, *109*(4). https://doi.org/10.1152/jn.00226.2012

Pesquita, A., Brennan, A., Enns, J. T., & Soto-Faraco, S. (2013). Isolating shape from semantics in haptic-visual priming. *Experimental Brain Research*, *227*(3), 311–22. https://doi.org/10.1007/s00221-013-3489-1

Proctor, R. W., & Lu, C.-H. (1999). Processing irrelevant location information: practice and transfer effects in choice-reaction tasks. *Memory & Cognition*, *27*(1), 63–77.

Puigcerver, L., Gonzalez-Contijoch, A., Nannen, P., Termes, M., Correa, G., Egea-Castillo, N., ... Navarra, J. (2018). Testing new strategies to reduce malnutrition in child and adolescent cancer patients under chemotherapy treatment. In *Joint Congress of SEPEX-SEPNECA-AIP, Madrid 3–6 July.* (p. 121). Madrid.

Quick, R. F. (1974). A vector-magnitude model of contrast detection. *Kybernetik*, *16*(2), 65–7. https://doi.org/10.1007/BF00271628

Reales, J. M., & Ballesteros, S. (1999). Implicit and explicit memory for visual and haptic objects: Cross-modal priming depends on structural descriptions. *Journal of Experimental Psychology: Learning, Memory, and Cognition*, *25*(3), 644.

Riggio, L., de Gonzaga Gawryszewski, L., & Umilta, C. (1986). What is crossed in crossed-hand effects? *Acta Psychologica*, *62*(1), 89–100.

Risko, E. F., Laidlaw, K., Freeth, M., Foulsham, T., & Kingstone, A. (2012). Social attention with real versus reel stimuli: toward an empirical approach to concerns about ecological validity. *Frontiers in Human Neuroscience*, *6*, 143. https://doi.org/10.3389/fnhum.2012.00143

Roa Romero, Y., Senkowski, D., & Keil, J. (2015). Early and late beta-band power reflect audiovisual perception in the McGurk illusion. *Journal of Neurophysiology*, *113*(7), 2342–50. https://doi.org/10.1152/jn.00783.2014

Roberts, K. L., & Hall, D. A. (2008). Examining a supramodal network for conflict processing: a systematic review and novel functional magnetic resonance imaging data for related visual and auditory stroop tasks. *Journal of Cognitive Neuroscience, 20*(6), 1063–78.

Rockland, K. S., & Ojima, H. (2003). Multisensory convergence in calcarine visual areas in macaque monkey. *International Journal of Psychophysiology, 50*(1–2), 19–26. https://doi.org/10.1016/S0167–8760(03)00121–1

Röder, B., Kusmierek, A., Spence, C., & Schicke, T. (2007). Developmental vision determines the reference frame for the multisensory control of action. *Proceedings of the National Academy of Sciences, 104*(11), 4753–8.

Rohe, T., & Noppeney, U. (2015). Cortical hierarchies perform Bayesian causal inference in multisensory perception. *PLOS Biology, 13*(2), e1002073. https://doi.org/10.1371/journal.pbio.1002073

Romei, V., Gross, J., & Thut, G. (2010). On the role of prestimulus alpha rhythms over occipito-parietal areas in visual input regulation: correlation or causation? *The Journal of Neuroscience, 30*(25), 8692 LP–8697.

Romei, V., Gross, J., & Thut, G. (2012). Sounds reset rhythms of visual cortex and corresponding human visual perception. *Current Biology, 22*(9), 807–13. https://doi.org/10.1016/J.CUB.2012.03.025

Romei, V., Murray, M. M., Cappe, C., & Thut, G. (2009). Preperceptual and stimulus-selective enhancement of low-level human visual cortex excitability by sounds. *Current Biology, 19*(21), 1799–805. https://doi.org/10.1016/J.CUB.2009.09.027

Roseboom, W., Kawabe, T., & Nishida, S. (2013). The cross-modal double flash illusion depends on featural similarity between cross-modal inducers. *Scientific Reports, 3*(1), 3437. https://doi.org/10.1038/srep03437

Roseboom, W., Nishida, S., Fujisaki, W., & Arnold, D. H. (2011). Audio-visual speech timing sensitivity is enhanced in cluttered conditions. *PLoS ONE, 6*(4), e18309. https://doi.org/10.1371/journal.pone.0018309

Ross, L. A., Saint-Amour, D., Leavitt, V. M., Javitt, D. C., & Foxe, J. J. (2006). Do you see what I am saying? Exploring visual enhancement of speech comprehension in noisy environments. *Cerebral Cortex, 17*(5), 1147–53. https://doi.org/10.1093/cercor/bhl024

Roswarski, T. E., & Proctor, R. W. (2000). Auditory stimulus-response compatibility: Is there a contribution of stimulus–hand correspondence? *Psychological Research, 63*(2), 148–58.

Rummukainen, O., Radun, J., Virtanen, T., & Pulkki, V. (2014). Categorization of natural dynamic audiovisual scenes. *PLoS ONE, 9*(5), e95848. https://doi.org/10.1371/journal.pone.0095848

Ruzzoli, M., & Soto-Faraco, S. (2014). Alpha stimulation of the human parietal cortex attunes tactile perception to external space. *Current Biology*, *24*(3). https://doi.org/10.1016/j.cub.2013.12.029

Ruzzoli, M., & Soto-Faraco, S. (2017). Modality-switching in the Simon task: the clash of reference frames. *Journal of Experimental Psychology: General*, *146*(10). https://doi.org/10.1037/xge0000342

Sams, M., Tiippana, K., Puharinen, H., & Möttönen, R. (2011). Sound location can influence audiovisual speech perception when spatial attention is manipulated. *Seeing and Perceiving*, *24*(1), 67–90. https://doi.org/10.1163/187847511X557308

Sánchez-García, C., Enns, J. T., & Soto-Faraco, S. (2013). Cross-modal prediction in speech depends on prior linguistic experience. *Experimental Brain Research*, *225*(4). https://doi.org/10.1007/s00221-012-3390-3

Sánchez-García, C., Kandel, S., Savariaux, C., & Soto-Faraco, S. (2018). The time course of audio-visual phoneme identification: a high temporal resolution study. *Multisensory Research*, *31*(1–2), 57–78. https://doi.org/10.1163/22134808-00002560

Santangelo, V., Di Francesco, S. A., Mastroberardino, S., & Macaluso, E. (2015). Parietal cortex integrates contextual and saliency signals during the encoding of natural scenes in working memory. *Human Brain Mapping*, *36*(12), 5003–17. https://doi.org/10.1002/hbm.22984

Santangelo, V., & Spence, C. (2007). Multisensory cues capture spatial attention regardless of perceptual load. *Journal of Experimental Psychology: Human Perception and Performance*, *33*(6), 1311–21. https://doi.org/10.1037/0096-1523.33.6.1311

Schneider, T. R., Engel, A. K., & Debener, S. (2008). Multisensory identification of natural objects in a two-way crossmodal priming paradigm. *Experimental Psychology*, *55*(2), 121–32. https://doi.org/10.1027/1618-3169.55.2.121

Schroeder, C. E., & Lakatos, P. (2009). Low-frequency neuronal oscillations as instruments of sensory selection. *Trends in Neurosciences*, *32*(1), 9–18. https://doi.org/10.1016/J.TINS.2008.0 9.012

Schroeder, C. E., Lakatos, P., Kajikawa, Y., Partan, S., & Puce, A. (2008). Neuronal oscillations and visual amplification of speech. *Trends in Cognitive Sciences*, *12*(3), 106–13. https://doi.org/10.1016/J.TICS.2008.0 1.002

Scott, J. J., & Gray, R. (2008). A comparison of tactile, visual, and auditory warnings for rear-end collision prevention in simulated driving. *Human Factors: The Journal of the Human Factors and Ergonomics Society*, *50*(2), 264–75. https://doi.org/10.1518/001872008X250674

Senkowski, D., Saint-Amour, D., Gruber, T., & Foxe, J. J. (2008). Look who's talking: the deployment of visuo-spatial attention during multisensory speech processing under noisy environmental conditions. *NeuroImage, 43*(2), 379–87. https://doi.org/10.1016/J.NEUROIMAGE.2008.0 6.046

Senkowski, D., Talsma, D., Herrmann, C. S., & Woldorff, M. G. (2005). Multisensory processing and oscillatory gamma responses: effects of spatial selective attention. *Experimental Brain Research, 166*(3–4), 411–26. https://doi.org/10.1007/s00221-005–2381–z

Shams, L., & Kim, R. (2010). Crossmodal influences on visual perception. *Physics of Life Reviews, 7*(3), 269–84. https://doi.org/10.1016/JPLREV .2010.0 4.006

Shams, L., & Seitz, A. R. (2008). Benefits of multisensory learning. *Trends in Cognitive Sciences, 12*(11), 411–17. https://doi.org/10.1016/J.TICS.2008.0 7.006

Shenhav, A., Botvinick, M. M., & Cohen, J. D. (2013). The expected value of control: an integrative theory of anterior cingulate cortex function. *Neuron, 79*(2), 217–40. https://doi.org/10.1016/J.NEURON.2013.0 7.007

Simon, J. R., Hinrichs, J. V, & Craft, J. L. (1970). Auditory SR compatibility: reaction time as a function of ear–hand correspondence and ear–response–location correspondence. *Journal of Experimental Psychology, 86*(1), 97–102.

Simon, J. R., & Small Jr, A. M. (1969). Processing auditory information: interference from an irrelevant cue. *Journal of Applied Psychology, 53*(5), 433.

Skipper, J. I. (2014). Echoes of the spoken past: how auditory cortex hears context during speech perception. *Philosophical Transactions of the Royal Society of London. Series B, Biological Sciences, 369*(1651), 20130297. https://doi.org/10.1098/rstb.2013.0297

Skipper, J. I., Goldin-Meadow, S., Nusbaum, H. C., & Small, S. L. (2009). Gestures orchestrate brain networks for language understanding. *Current Biology, 19*(8), 661–7. https://doi.org/10.1016/J.CUB.2009.02.051

Skipper, J. I., Van Wassenhove, V., Nusbaum, H. C., & Small, S. L. (2007). Hearing lips and seeing voices: how cortical areas supporting speech production mediate audiovisual speech perception. *Cerebral Cortex, 17*(10), 2387–99.

Smilek, D., Birmingham, E., Cameron, D., Bischof, W., & Kingstone, A. (2006). Cognitive ethology and exploring attention in real-world scenes. *Brain Research, 1080*(1), 101–19. https://doi.org/10.1016/J.BRAINRES.2005.1 2.090

Smilek, D., Eastwood, J. D., Reynolds, M. G., & Kingstone, A. (2007). Metacognitive errors in change detection: missing the gap between lab and life. *Consciousness and Cognition, 16*(1), 52–7. https://doi.org/10.1016/J .CONCOG.2006.04.001

Smith, R. E., MacKenzie, S. B., Yang, X., Buchholz, L. M., & Darley, W. K. (2007). Modeling the determinants and effects of creativity in advertising. *Marketing Science, 26*(6), 819–33.

So, W. C., Sim Chen-Hui, C., & Low Wei-Shan, J. (2012). Mnemonic effect of iconic gesture and beat gesture in adults and children: is meaning in gesture important for memory recall? *Language and Cognitive Processes, 27*(5), 665–81. https://doi.org/10.1080/01690965.2011.573220

Soto-Faraco, S., Morein-Zamir, S., & Kingstone, A. (2005). On audiovisual spatial synergy: the fragility of the phenomenon, *Perception & Psychophysics, 67*(3), 444–57. https://doi.org/10.3758/BF03193323

Soto-Faraco, S., Navarra, J., & Alsius, A. (2004). Assessing automaticity in audiovisual speech integration: evidence from the speeded classification task. *Cognition, 92*(3), B13–B23. https://doi.org/10.1016/j.cognition.2003.10.005

Spence, C. (2011). Crossmodal correspondences: A tutorial review. *Attention, Perception, & Psychophysics, 73*(4), 971–95. https://doi.org/10.3758/s13414-010-0073-7

Spence, C. (2016). Multisensory packaging design: color, shape, texture, sound, and smell. In P. Burgess (Ed.), *Integrating the packaging and product experience in food and beverages: a road-map to consumer satisfaction* (pp. 1–22). Woodhead Publishing. https://doi.org/10.1016/B978-0-08-100356-5.00001-2

Spence, C. (2018). Multisensory perception. In J. Wixed (Ed.-in-chief) & J. Serences (Vol. Ed.) (Eds.), *Stevens' handbook of experimental psychology and cognitive neuroscience* (4th ed., pp. 1–56). Hoboken, NJ: John Wiley & Sons, Inc. https://doi.org/10.1002/9781119170174.epcn214

Spence, C., & Driver, J. (2004). *Crossmodal space and crossmodal attention.* Oxford University Press.

Spence, C., & Ho, C. (2008). Tactile and multisensory spatial warning signals for drivers. *IEEE Transactions on Haptics, 1*(2), 121–9. https://doi.org/10.1109/TOH.2008.14

Spence, C., & Ho, C. (2015a). Crossmodal attention: from the laboratory to the real world (and back again). In J. M. Fawcet, E. F. Risko, & A. Kingstone (eds.), *The handbook of attention* (pp. 119–38). Cambridge, MA: Massachusetts Institute of Technology Press.

Spence, C., & Ho, C. (2015b). Multisensory information processing. In D. A. Boehm-Davis, F. T. Durso, & J. D. Lee (eds.), *APA handbook of human systems integration* (pp. 435–48). Washington: American Psychological Association. https://doi.org/10.1037/14528-027

Spence, C., & Santangelo, V. (2009). Capturing spatial attention with multisensory cues: a review. *Hearing Research, 258*(1–2), 134–42. https://doi.org/10.1016/j.heares.2009.04.015

Spence, C., & Soto-Faraco, S. (in press). Crossmodal attention applied: lessons for/from driving. In M. Chun (Ed.), *Cambridge elements of attention.* Cambridge, UK: Cambridge University Press.

Spence, C., & Squire, S. (2003). Multisensory integration: maintaining the perception of synchrony. *Current Biology, 13*(13), R519–R521. https://doi .org/10.1016/S0960-9822(03)00445-7

Spiers, H. J., & Maguire, E. A. (2006). Thoughts, behaviour, and brain dynamics during navigation in the real world. *NeuroImage, 31*(4), 1826–40. https://doi.org/10.1016/J.NEUROIMAGE.2006.01.037

Stein, B. E. (Ed.). (2012). *The new handbook of multisensory processes.* Cambridge, MA: Massachusetts Institute of Technology Press.

Stein, B. E., London, N., Wilkinson, L. K., & Price, D. D. (1996). Enhancement of perceived visual intensity by auditory stimuli: a psychophysical analysis. *Journal of Cognitive Neuroscience, 8*(6), 497–506. https://doi.org/10.1162 /jocn.1996.8.6.497

Stein, B. E., & Meredith, M. A. (1993). *The merging of the senses.* Cambridge, MA: Massachusetts Institute of Technology Press.

Stein, B. E., & Stanford, T. R. (2008). Multisensory integration: current issues from the perspective of the single neuron. *Nature Reviews Neuroscience, 9*(4), 255–66. https://doi.org/10.1038/nrn2331

Stekelenburg, J. J., & Vroomen, J. (2007). Neural correlates of multisensory integration of ecologically valid audiovisual events. *Journal of Cognitive Neuroscience, 19*(12), 1964–73. https://doi.org/10.1162/jocn.2007.19.12 .1964

Stekelenburg, J. J., & Vroomen, J. (2012). Electrophysiological correlates of predictive coding of auditory location in the perception of natural audiovisual events. *Frontiers in Integrative Neuroscience, 6*, 26.

Stoffer, T. H. (1991). Attentional focussing and spatial stimulus-response compatibility. *Psychological Research, 53*(2), 127–35.

Stroop, J. R. (1935). Studies of interference in serial verbal reactions. *Journal of Experimental Psychology, 18*(6), 643–62. https://doi.org/10.1037/h0054651

Suied, C., Bonneel, N., & Viaud-Delmon, I. (2009). Integration of auditory and visual information in the recognition of realistic objects. *Experimental Brain Research, 194*(1), 91–102. https://doi.org/10.1007/s00221-008-1672-6

Sumby, W. H., & Pollack, I. (1954). Visual contribution to speech intelligibility in noise. *The Journal of the Acoustical Society of America, 26*(2), 212–15. https://doi.org/10.1121/1.1907309

Szycik, G. R., Jansma, H., & Münte, T. F. (2009). Audiovisual integration during speech comprehension: an fMRI study comparing ROI-based and whole brain analyses. *Human Brain Mapping, 30*(7), 1990–9.

Talsma, D. (2015). Predictive coding and multisensory integration: an attentional account of the multisensory mind. *Frontiers in Integrative Neuroscience, 09*, 19. https://doi.org/10.3389/fnint.2015.00019

Talsma, D., Doty, T. J., & Woldorff, M. G. (2006). Selective attention and audiovisual integration: is attending to both modalities a prerequisite for early integration? *Cerebral Cortex*, *17*(3), 679–90. https://doi.org/10.1093/cercor/bhk016

Talsma, D., Senkowski, D., Soto-Faraco, S., & Woldorff, M. G. (2010). The multifaceted interplay between attention and multisensory integration. *Trends in Cognitive Sciences*, *14*(9), 400–10. https://doi.org/10.1016/j.tics.2010.06.008

Talsma, D., & Woldorff, M. G. (2005). Selective attention and multisensory integration: multiple phases of effects on the evoked brain activity. *Journal of Cognitive Neuroscience*, *17*(7), 1098–114. https://doi.org/10.1162/0898929054475172

ten Oever, S., Romei, V., van Atteveldt, N., Soto-Faraco, S., Murray, M. M., & Matusz, P. J. (2016). The COGs (context, object, and goals) in multisensory processing. *Experimental Brain Research*, *234*(5). https://doi.org/10.1007/s00221-016-4590-z

Thorne, J. D., De Vos, M., Viola, F. C., & Debener, S. (2011). Cross-modal phase reset predicts auditory task performance in humans. *The Journal of Neuroscience: The Official Journal of the Society for Neuroscience*, *31*(10), 3853–3861. https://doi.org/10.1523/JNEUROSCI.6176-10.2011

Thut, G., Veniero, D., Romei, V., Miniussi, C., Schyns, P., & Gross, J. (2011). Rhythmic TMS causes local entrainment of natural oscillatory signatures. *Current Biology*, *21*(14), 1176–85. https://doi.org/10.1016/J.CUB.2011.05.049

Tiippana, K. (2014). What is the McGurk effect? *Frontiers in Psychology*, *5*, 725.

Tiippana, K., Andersen, T. S., & Sams, M. (2004). Visual attention modulates audiovisual speech perception. *European Journal of Cognitive Psychology*, *16*(3), 457–72. https://doi.org/10.1080/09541440340000268

Umiltà, C., & Liotti, M. (1987). Egocentric and relative spatial codes in SR compatibility. *Psychological Research*, *49*(2–3), 81–90.

Urbantschitsch, V. (1880). Beobachtungen über centrale Acusticusaffectionen. *Archiv Für Ohrenheilkunde*, *16*(3), 171–87.

van Atteveldt, N., Murray, M. M., Thut, G., & Schroeder, C. E. (2014). Multisensory integration: flexible use of general operations. *Neuron*, *81*(6), 1240–53. https://doi.org/10.1016/J.NEURON.2014.02.044

van de Par, S., & Kohlrausch, A. (2004). Visual and auditory object selection based on temporal correlations between auditory and visual cues. In *18th Int. Congress on Acoustics* (pp. 4–9). Kyoto.

Van Der Burg, E., Olivers, C. N. L., Bronkhorst, A. W., & Theeuwes, J. (2008). Pip and pop: nonspatial auditory signals improve spatial visual search.

Journal of Experimental Psychology: Human Perception and Performance, *34*(5), 1053–65. https://doi.org/10.1037/0096–1523.34.5.1053

Van der Burg, E., Talsma, D., Olivers, C. N. L., Hickey, C., & Theeuwes, J. (2011). Early multisensory interactions affect the competition among multiple visual objects. *NeuroImage, 55*(3), 1208–18. https://doi.org/10.1016/J .NEUROIMAGE.2010.12.068

van Wassenhove, V., Grant, K. W., & Poeppel, D. (2005). Visual speech speeds up the neural processing of auditory speech. *Proceedings of the National Academy of Sciences of the United States of America, 102*(4), 1181–6. https:// doi.org/10.1073/pnas.0408949102

van Wassenhove, V., Grant, K. W., & Poeppel, D. (2007). Temporal window of integration in auditory-visual speech perception. *Neuropsychologia, 45*(3), 598–607. https://doi.org/10.1016/J.NEUROPSYCHOLOGIA.2006.01.001

Varela, F., Toro, A., John, E., & Schwartz, E. (1981). Perceptual framing and cortical alpha rhythm. *Neuropsychologia,* 19:5.

Vatakis, A., & Spence, C. (2006). Audiovisual synchrony perception for music, speech, and object actions. *Brain Research, 1111*(1), 134–42. https://doi.org /10.1016/J.BRAINRES.2006.05.078

Vatakis, A., & Spence, C. (2007). Crossmodal binding: evaluating the 'unity assumption' using audiovisual speech stimuli. *Perception & Psychophysics, 69*(5), 744–56. https://doi.org/10.3758/BF03193776

Vercillo, T., Tonelli, A., Goodale, M., & Gori, M. (2017). Restoring an allocentric reference frame in blind individuals through echolocation. *The Journal of the Acoustical Society of America, 141*(5), 3453. https://doi.org/10 .1121/1.4987160

Vroomen, J., Bertelson, P., & de Gelder, B. (2001). Directing spatial attention towards the illusory location of a ventriloquized sound. *Acta Psychologica, 108*(1), 21–33. https://doi.org/10.1016/S0001–6918(00)00068–8

Vroomen, J., & Gelder, B. de. (2000). Sound enhances visual perception: Crossmodal effects of auditory organization on vision. *Journal of Experimental Psychology: Human Perception and Performance.* American Psychological Association. https://doi.org/10.1037/0096–1523.26.5.1583

Vroomen, J., & Keetels, M. (2010). Perception of intersensory synchrony: a tutorial review. *Attention, Perception, & Psychophysics, 72*(4), 871–84. https://doi.org/10.3758/APP.72.4.871

Wallace, R. J. (1972). Spatial SR compatibility effects involving kinesthetic cues. *Journal of Experimental Psychology, 93*(1), 163–8.

Ward, L. M. (2002). *Dynamical cognitive science.* Cambridge, MA: Massachussetts Institute of Technology Press.

Weissman, D. H., Giesbrecht, B., Song, A. W., Mangun, G. R., & Woldorff, M. G. (2003). Conflict monitoring in the human anterior cingulate cortex during selective attention to global and local object features. *Neuroimage, 19*(4), 1361–8.

Welch, R. B. (1999). Chapter 15: meaning, attention, and the 'unity assumption' in the intersensory bias of spatial and temporal perceptions. *Advances in Psychology, 129,* 371–87. https://doi.org/10.1016/S0166–4115(99)80036–3

Welch, R. B., DuttonHurt, L. D., & Warren, D. H. (1986). Contributions of audition and vision to temporal rate perception. *Perception & Psychophysics, 39*(4), 294–300. https://doi.org/10.3758/BF03204939

Wiggs, C. L., & Martin, A. (1998). Properties and mechanisms of perceptual priming. *Current Opinion in Neurobiology, 8,* 227–33.

Wolfe, J. M., Horowitz, T. S., & Kenner, N. M. (2005). Rare items often missed in visual searches. *Nature, 435*(7041), 439–40. https://doi.org/10.1038/435439a

Wu, C.-C., Wick, F. A., & Pomplun, M. (2014). Guidance of visual attention by semantic information in real-world scenes. *Frontiers in Psychology, 5,* 54. https://doi.org/10.3389/fpsyg.2014.00054

Yamamoto, S., & Kitazawa, S. (2001). Reversal of subjective temporal order due to arm crossing. *Nature Neuroscience, 4,* 759–65.

Yarrow, K., Roseboom, W., & Arnold, D. H. (2011). Spatial grouping resolves ambiguity to drive temporal recalibration. *Journal of Experimental Psychology. Human Perception and Performance, 37*(5), 1657–61. https://doi.org/10.1037/a0024235

Yau, J. M., Olenczak, J. B., Dammann, J. F., & Bensmaia, S. J. (2009). Temporal frequency channels are linked across audition and touch. *Current Biology, 19*(7), 561–6. https://doi.org/10.1016/J.CUB.2009.02.013

Zion Golumbic, E. M., Ding, N., Bickel, S., Lakatos, P., Schevon, C. A., McKhann, G. M., ... Schroeder, C. E. (2013). Mechanisms underlying selective neuronal tracking of attended speech at a 'cocktail party'. *Neuron, 77*(5), 980–91. https://doi.org/10.1016/J.NEURON.2012.12.037

Acknowledgements

This research was supported by the Ministerio de Economía y Competitividad (PSI2016-75558-P AEI/FEDER), AGAUR Generalitat de Catalunya (2017 SGR 1545), and the European Research Council (StG-2010 263145). M. R. was supported by a Juan de la Cierva postdoctoral fellowship (JCI-2012–12335) from the Ministerio de Economía y Competitividad. D. K. was supported by an FI scholarship from AGAUR – Generalitat de Catalunya.

Cambridge Elements $\equiv$

Perception

James T. Enns
The University of British Columbia

Editor James T. Enns is Professor at the University of British Columbia, where he researches the interaction of perception, attention, emotion, and social factors. He has previously been Editor of the *Journal of Experimental Psychology: Human Perception and Performance* and an Associate Editor at *Psychological Science, Consciousness and Cognition, Attention Perception & Psychophysics,* and *Visual Cognition*.

Editorial Board

About the Series

The modern study of human perception includes event perception, bidirectional influences between perception and action, music, language, the integration of the senses, human action observation, and the important roles of emotion, motivation, and social factors. Each Element in the series combines authoritative literature reviews of foundational topics with forward-looking presentations of the recent developments on a given topic.

Cambridge Elements ≡

Perception

Elements in the Series

Hypothesis Testing Reconsidered
Gregory Francis

Chemical Senses in Feeding, Belonging, and Surviving:
Or, Are You Going to Eat That?
Paul A. S. Breslin

Multisensory Interactions in the Real World
Salvador Soto-Faraco, Daria Kvasova, Emmanuel Biau, Nara Ikumi,
Manuela Ruzzoli, Luis Morís-Fernández and Mireia Torralba

A full series listing is available at: www.cambridge.org/EPER

Printed in the United States
By Bookmasters